TABLE OF CONTENTS

DEDICATION

Ron, thank you for your unending love and constant support. You told me to write the first story. I did. Then you said to write the second.... Thank you for taking my car to work every Monday and bringing dinner home every Monday night. That forced me to stay home and focus. You have sacrificed so much for so many. Don't think God won't reward all of it. It has been such an honor to serve God as your wife. I love you, my forever best friend. My cup overflows.

Becky and Scott, thank you for being amazing people. You are kind, smart, loving, and hilarious. How you have blessed our marriage. It has been such a privilege to be your mother and friend. You have enriched my life in every way imaginable and then some. As I recall all the miles we have traveled on this journey called life, I am overcome with emotion (shocking, I know) at how very blessed I am to have you both. May you continue to be storytellers in your families. I love you equally and deeply.

I must thank Mammy, who is long gone, for starting what she could never imagine: my book. And for Mom and Dad who modeled extravagant parenting and made my life so full and fun. I was incredibly blessed to be your daughter.

Carole, Gordon, and Joanne, you are the *best* siblings God ever could have given to me. Thanks for doing life with me since the very beginning. I love you all.

Emma Clark, thank you for completing my stories with your incredible gift of editing. You are amazing.

And thanks be to God for saving my soul and blessing me with thousands of friends over the decades — some people whom I may not remember by name but whom I had a season with. You made my life run over with gladness. Relationships enrich me, and there are simply too many to count.

INTRODUCTION

M y earliest memories of storytelling came from my grandmother's backyard. My maternal grandmother was born in Sweden and boarded a ship sailing to America in 1905, chasing the man she loved. She caught Papa, married him, learned English, and mothered seven children. Life was difficult for her, and times were tough. One of her favorite pastimes was hosting her Swedish lady friends for coffee and pastries. After their home chores were completed, these older women grabbed their folding chairs and came to Mammy's backyard for fellowship. They spoke easily in their native tongue. They could say anything—and get away with it—as no one except them knew Swedish. They would chat for hours and find renewal and healing in friendship and laughter.

Coffee (*kaffe*) was the key ingredient in each of those afternoons. Every woman would anticipate a hot, strong brew from their friend and neighbor, "Nettie." And she never disappointed. Mammy would serve cup after cup to woman after woman, asking, "Would you like more coffee?" ("*Skulle du vilja mer kaffe?*") At about cup number three or four, the ladies would always respond with "*Fem droppar*," which literally means five drops. So my grandmother would pour only a half cup, and the afternoon would slowly come to a close.

The name of this book originates from those many gatherings and the phrase that was carried down to my mother's generation and mine and now my kids. We have used that phrase in every conceivable occasion — when it fits and when it doesn't: with coffee, water, juice, second helpings of dessert, and any other time we just want a little bit of something. We love this phrase, and it keeps us close to those we have lost for a time.

Up until mother's ninety-third year, she would only want "fem droppar" of something, and it was fully understood, and we complied.

Jesus told stories all the time. He instructs the masses by using the things people know or can relate to. He makes the points He desires to make, as He is the Master storyteller. Of course His are supreme, because He is God.

When life was slower and simpler, people would sit a spell, tell stories, and enjoy being together. The fast-paced society of today is missing that special gift of time and the art of storytelling. We must reclaim it. What my parents didn't share with me orally is now gone. I am so grateful Mom and Dad told us stories. They helped us define who we were and where we came from. Telling and retelling stories to the next generations must be of greater importance, I believe. That's why I wrote this book.

These stories are all true; only a few names have been changed for protection. The stories I have chosen are particularly for my children, Becky and Scott, so that some of our memories will be preserved.

So, get yourself "fem droppar" of coffee, tea, lemonade, or water and enjoy a story or two. May you be encouraged, challenged, inspired, convicted, blessed, or influenced to write your own stories down. Here's to some stories of faith, family, and fun.

MY REVOLUTIONARY WAR
(circa 1972)

Once upon a time there was a young maiden named Nancy. She lived in a place steeped in history, right down the street from where the first battle of the Revolutionary War was fought. In 1775, Paul Revere rode on horseback right down the street where she lived, warning the Lexington Minutemen, "The British are coming! The British are coming!" April 19, the day of the Battles of Lexington and Concord, is still commemorated in Massachusetts by celebrating Patriots' Day. No school. Parades. People enjoying their freedom because a war was fought and won.

One year she was invited to go on a double date with her favorite neighbor, Linda. She had no idea who her date would be but was over the moon that they would be going to "The Revolutionary Reenactment." Even though it was less than a mile from her house, she had somehow never gotten around to attending.

In anticipation of the fun, historic, one-of-a-kind evening, she set off to find the most beautiful dress in all the land. She spent night and day looking until she found it. It was a long, cotton dress with many layers. The muted hues were perfect. The added feature of an apron-like front made it the ideal period dress she was looking for. The sleeves were long, and lace covered the entire forearm. When she slipped it on, she felt like George Washington himself could be escorting her.

The afternoon of the big day finally arrived. She was dressed early, excited to be part of the reenactment of an event she had only read about in history books. Finally, the doorbell rang. She almost ran to the front door of their beautiful colonial home but remembered she was a lady and slowly walked to greet her date. Much to her joy, a handsome man with a wig, smartly dressed in fashionable knickers and proper attire, greeted her in his British accent. This night was going to be the best. And off they went.

Dinner was held at a famous inn nearby for all the actors and dates. The fare was delicious and historically accurate. Linda and Nancy left the dinner for a brief time to try to have a smoke break, but were stopped immediately by some brute who disgustedly rebuked, "Women don't smoke!" They were ushered back to their seats, quietly grumbling, "Man, these actors take this gig a little seriously, don't they?" And so the dissatisfied but obedient maidens sat with their darling men, making small talk and looking fantastic.

After dinner, they traveled to the Battle Green. The scene was incredible. Real cannons, real soldiers, real smoke (good thing the cannons weren't females) and great narratives given about the sacrifices made and victories won. It made Nancy so proud to be a free American.

Her date had been the perfect gentleman, acting the part of a British Redcoat. And she had been the well-dressed, well-mannered (except for the smoking incident) dignified dame. With the acting part behind them, Nancy was now interested in finding out more about her date. Her escort asked her, in his beautifully British accent, if she would like to go to his place. Because it was 1972, when life seemed so much simpler, and he had been such an upstanding, outstanding, polished, and refined man of honor, she said, "Yes."

While he was dressed in his costume, he still kept on with the British accent. It was the only "him" she knew, and they conversed while he drove to the next town, his hometown. When they reached his apartment, he asked if he might "change into something a little more comfortable." She assured him that she understood being dressed in his old-fashioned attire for so many hours must have been a tough assignment. She, on the other hand, felt comfortable and elegant all night. No tight-fitting jacket, no wig, no odd-shaped shoes. "Please get comfortable," she insisted. And off he went, the last she saw of her British lord .

When his bedroom door opened, Nancy stood in disbelief. There, positioned in front of her, was a man in a smoking jacket. Yuck. Wig gone. Greasy black hair slicked back. Sloppy and sickening. Even his smile changed. *Is this the same guy? Bring back the phony Brit. Please.*

Without further discussion, she asked to be taken home. Not a word was spoken between them ever again. And she lived happily after without him.

I have reflected on this story throughout the years and wondered how many people in life resort to acting instead of just being who they are from the beginning. Wouldn't it make more sense and be easier on everyone just to be ourselves and love who God made? What is so hard about that?

The shame of this story is that when I met the "real guy," I thought of him as disgusting. I kinda fell for the "fake." When the real him was revealed, he could not possibly match the proper Englishman with class, position, and attire. I didn't see it coming—and then I felt bad that I was so rude. I think I was in shock. A smoking jacket? Are you serious? Lesson: Just be yourself and love yourself. God does. And never consider a smoking jacket.

NATASHA LEIBENFROST

We had just returned home from Europe, where I had completed my senior year in an international school, just outside of Frankfurt, Germany. I was pretty good at speaking German in those days.

When I got my license at age nineteen, I remember going with my father to buy my very first car, right from the showroom floor: a 1972 shiny, red VW Beetle. I would pay every red cent, but my father would co-sign for me, as I had no credit history to speak of. I promptly bought myself a white decal with the letter D for the back of my new car, claiming Deutschland. I was transitioning back to the American lifestyle, except for one little area: being confined to speed limits. During my days and nights on the German autobahn, where there was no limit, it just seemed reasonable. Youth.

One sunny afternoon, I was traveling south on Route 128 in Massachusetts at about 95 mph. Oops. A police officer was parked on the side of the road, waiting for offenders. Got one. Ahhhhh! Guilty. I slowed to a stop in about eleven miles (hey, it takes a while to stop at that speed). Busted.

As the officer approached my window, he was *not* happy to see me. He firmly asked to see my license and registration, to which I flippantly responded in German, "*Bitte?*" which simply means, "Come again?" Inwardly, I wondered where on earth it came from. Sadly, it comes from within all of us at times we are backed into a corner. Call it what it is: sin. And it lurks in every heart on the planet. He looked at me, slowed his speech, and clearly enunciated his command once again, "Please. Give. Me. Your. License. And. Registration." I had a decision to make — quickly. Lie, or probably go to jail. So, I chose the lie, which came much easier for me. He asked me what my name was, again in that slow manner. I parroted back to him, again in German, "*Meine* name?" And if you can even believe this: I blurted out the name Natasha Leibenfrost! If you think I am up into the night thinking of false identifications for myself, you would be dead wrong. *Holy smokes! If this guy finds out my real name is Nancy Sullivan from Boston, I am a cooked goose.* So the little charade continued, as I tried to win him with good German, nice smiles, and great inflection. I was too idiotic to have a trace of nerves back then.

He did not know how to ticket a foreigner, so he turned to walk away. I heard his final reaction under his breath: "**blank** foreigners." And with that I was free. I don't think I ever hit 95 mph again. Maturity has great benefits.

CROSS COUNTRY

D on't you just love America? I am so proud to be an American citizen. God shed His grace on thee. I love patriotic parades. I love our military. I love our flag. I love our anthem. I will stand beside her and pray God guides her through the night with light from above. We have been handed a rich (and costly) legacy, and I intend to do my small part to keep America great.

Having sung the many great patriotic songs all my life, I desired to see the amber waves of grain and the purple mountain majesties above the fruited plain. I absolutely needed to drive from sea to shining sea, and so I did — a few times.

The first drive was done solo in a 1966 green convertible VW with handmade green plaid slipcovers. It was the coolest car (in my estimation) anywhere in the northeast. My plan was to work temporary secretarial jobs until I had enough money to get from Boston to Denver to visit my sister and her husband. Every temp job I worked extended a permanent offer; no one was getting that I was *leaving* and heading out west. New turf. New adventures. New relationships. New everything. I was yearning to depart New England, and now was the time.

Mile by mile, song by song, state by state we covered 2,000 miles, my car and me. The truck drivers were such a help back then. They were informed, friendly, and very helpful. Pulling over in truck stops proved to be amusing, as we all recognized one another. Just driving down highway after highway, looking out for each other. It was a glorious adventure.

When I arrived at Carole's, it was such a pleasure to visit and catch up on things we had missed out on in each other's lives. My brother-in-law, Dave, gave the car the "once-over" and found that the battery was sitting on a very, very thin, rusted fragment of metal. There had been only a fraction of metal between the car battery and the road. When I saw the lack of flooring, I was amazed I had driven such a distance with such false confidence.

When you are confronted with something of this magnitude, you are required to make a move. I sold the car to someone else who was better equipped to bring things to a higher safety standard. Mostly, the selling features were the seat covers, which were gorgeous, and the fact that it was summer and a convertible was the way to go.

The Bible records a line in the Book of Judges that I find comforting after that trek: "Go in peace. The Lord is watching over the journey you are going on" (18:6).

MR. SULLIVAN OF BOSTON

Years ago my brother, Gordon, was working as head sommelier at a five-star hotel. Our father decided to fly from Boston to Florida to visit his son and encourage him. He put aside all reason and decided to dine in the swanky restaurant. Gordon immediately greeted his father in formal fashion and got him the finest of wines to begin the experience.

The restaurant started filling up one table at a time until the dining room was full. Friends of Gordon heard that "Dad" was in town, so everyone wanted to meet Gordon's father. One by one his co-workers would stop by Dad's table and introduce themselves and share a comment or two about their relationship with his son. Dad found the people very receptive to his being there and enjoyed meeting all of his son's new acquaintances.

So you understand, most of the clientele who visit this particular place claim celebrity status. If you want to catch a glimpse of a movie star, this is one of the places you would go— if you could afford it. It truly was a top-shelf dining experience.

Some of the people in the dining room noticed the huge amount of people who were gracing Dad's table and became fixated on who he might be (He did favor Jimmy Stewart, I must say) After a long while of watching, but being too far from hearing the comments, one table just *had* to know who this guy was. The gentleman stopped the maître d' and asked who the guy was. The host looked in the direction of the questioning guest's finger pointing, saw Gordon's father, and simply responded, "Oh, that's Mr. Sullivan of Boston."

I have no doubt that couple spent the rest of that evening meal trying to figure out who Mr. Sullivan of Boston could be. A designer perhaps? A prized writer? A director? Nope, an invested father. That's all. That was always one of Dad's favorite stories.

SUMO AND SAL

When my father retired, he and mom moved to Hawaii. Well, of course the two younger kids joined them. It was slow-paced living with warmer temperatures. Mom and Dad were so deserving of that lifestyle. Mom would look for puka shells by day, and Dad would golf, read, or rest. It was very enjoyable for all.

My girlfriend from school flew over to join the party. There was no way she was enduring another cold New England winter while her friend was going to the beach every day. We secured an apartment and jobs.

I was working as a waitress in an upscale hotel for a time. I loved going to work for four hours and making more money in tips than a regular job would pay, had I given them eight hours of my time. I was living with my best friend, Sandy, close to the ocean and a few miles from work. Life was great.

One morning, word came that the manager of our apartment complex, Sumo, had killed Sam, the lifeguard at my hotel. I knew, liked, and respected both men. One was now dead and the other was apprehended and charged with murder.

They were trying Sumo for premeditated murder, as he planned things out by parking his vehicle at an adjacent complex and walked to his self-created crime site.

His path late that night was right past the apartment where my sister and I were celebrating a friend's birthday. After being questioned by the police, I was subpoenaed to testify that I had seen him walk past the window, which I had.

I met with the prosecuting attorney, and we went over all the questions and points he would be executing in this case and tried to anticipate what approach the counsel of the defendant might use to intimidate me. One instruction he gave me was not to look at the accused, just at my advocate at all times. Keeping it professional and keeping the emotions out of things, I guess is what he was hoping for.

My day in court had arrived. My nerves were shot as I entered the building. Knees were knocking, heart was pounding, and my mind was filled with fear. Would the killer think I was a tattletale? That I was here on my own volition? That I wanted him convicted? Yikes! This was a hard place for a young kid to find herself. Then I saw the support I needed to get through this horrible ordeal: my boyfriend, Ron. He was an officer of the law, and he was there to support me. As soon as I saw him, I knew things would be okay.

As I entered the courtroom, I did the unimaginable, the unintended, the unthinkable, the unplanned: I looked directly at Sumo and *waved*! As carefully scripted as things were, I could not believe my own behavior. What on earth had I just done? I engaged with him instead of ignoring him. Sometimes you just can't change things. Ditzy is as ditzy does! My attorney went forward, as if nothing had happened, keeping everything inside himself.

I was ripped by the defense attorney, as I had been warned I would be. His questioning began with the timing of things. "What time did you arrive at the party? When did you see him walk by the window? Are you sure it was prior to midnight?"

I dutifully answered, "It was 11:40 PM."

He further questioned, "Could it have been 11:45 PM?"

"Well yes, I suppose it could have been 11:45 PM," I responded.

And he kept pushing me. "Could it have been 11:50 PM?"

"No, it was not 11:50 PM" I replied.

He asked, "Why couldn't it have been 11:50 PM?"

"Because my father asked me to have my sister home by midnight, and I know I would have her home by then," was my comeback.

"What kind of watch do you wear?"

Are you serious? "I have a Timex," was my retort.

"Is it self-winding?"

No way! This guy is crazy! He finally dropped it, and I was most assuredly done with my assignment.

In the weeks that followed the trial, Sumo was released on bail, awaiting sentencing. He was found guilty and would be heading to prison soon. Life moved on.

One night I drove to my boyfriend's living quarters to see him before he worked his third shift assignment. The owner of a beautiful abandoned hotel had offered free rent to four officers if they would look after the property for him. What a sweet deal. The only problem was that there was no lighting on the premises after dark. My headlights led me safely up the hill to the old hotel. When I turned the car off, the black-ness of the night, reflected by the black lava rocks all around, would give way to my autonomous, self-directing skills to get to his door. There was no assistance from creation after the sun went down. It was exactly eighty-five steps to the northwest of where my car always parked; I had measured it by day and knew the path with full accuracy. I would sidestep the pool, the bushes, the plentiful lava rock, and I would see my beloved.

As I closed my car door, and said goodbye to all illumina-tion for a few moments, I heard someone say, "Nancy!" Who on earth was out here? I could not see the hand in front of my face. I didn't even know I had a face. I was summoned again. As I gazed in the direction of the voice calling to me, I saw a teeny tiny little light in the way distance (opposite from where the hotel was) and heard the voice clarify, "It's Sumo!" *Whaaaaat?* He asked for me to come to him. I have heard of people walking toward the light, but it usually meant to the hereafter. Well, I was walking toward a murderer. *I may end up in Heaven tonight after all!* I kept walking toward the flick-ering flame, and away from all that was familiar, even though everything familiar was cloaked in darkness. My proficient officer, somewhere to my left, was totally unaware of what was going on.

As I approached Sumo, I saw a killer with a knife. But the knife was being used appropriately; he was cleaning fish he had caught earlier in the day, enjoying his last few days of freedom. I knew the nice side of this fellow, so I listened to his utterance. In his Pidgin accent he simply said, "I been looking da whole island fa you." *Ahhhhhhhh! I knew it; he's ticked off I*

26

spoke at the trial. Sorry, buddy; it's the law, Gotta obey. And then his follow-up comment made me feel safe again. "I just like say I sorry fa putting you tru all dat!" He was apologizing. *That's the Sumo I know!* He knew he'd made a huge error in judgment and would serve years in restitution. And he was sorry he put me through the legal process .

Forgiveness came easy that night. "No problem. Gotta run to my *cop boyfriend* now. See you around." And back into the darkness I went. No light to guide me back. I might be hiking until daylight or drown in the pool. But I was headed in the opposite direction of that knife. If I could only find my car again…

CRACK SEED

C rack seed is a terrible candy, in my opinion. The locals in Hawaii love seeds; my husband grew up on them. Imagine this: a pit of a plum with an added exterior of wet or dry licorice wrapped around it. That's it. No wonder they come in bags of twenty-five or so, because one could never satisfy. They come in many varieties and are as common as chocolate candy bars are here on the mainland.

Through the years I have tried many of these novelties, but with little success. Ron and his brother, Bobby, were enjoying crack (the Pidgin way of speaking does not permit you to put an "-ed" on words like this) seed one time. I decided to try this "gem" and found it to be the worst variation of all. Take that plum seed, hammer it into fifty tiny pieces, and permit the licorice to hold all these small fragments of hard sharp edges together, and place one in your mouth. Who on earth would desire this? For someone to enjoy this experience, I think it requires a special skill that I do not possess. Your tongue (never your hands) must have the dexterity to separate the enjoyable candy from these many miserable shards. After a hard sliver has been detached from the sweet candy, spewing it to the ground is the next step. Please. I just don't get this, but then again, I wasn't raised in this culture.

Ron and his brother, Bobby, could talk, chew, and spit pits as sharp as broken glass while enjoying these "candies" and carrying on a conversation in a perfect balancing act. I never heard of any seed being swallowed by mistake. Unbelievable! What a talented twosome.

Then I had a sensational thought: I would bring some of these delicacies back to my friends. My first victim was my boss, Mack. I walked into his sizable office, complete with a massive window overlooking the bustling city of Atlanta, and gave this precious executive a crack seed with no explanation. Oh, how I wish you could have been there with us; I nearly lost my job.

Mack welcomed me back, asked about our trip, and put this devilish prank into his unsuspecting mouth. I rejoiced as I *knew* his tongue did not possess the skill needed to handle what was about to happen. He began the obvious chewing process that one would initiate when placing something in his mouth, never dreaming his faithful Girl Friday would have given him something with sharp pieces in it without a warning. In a flash he bit on a hard piece of seed, then several. His mouth was full of them now, as the licorice was releasing them.

You will not even consider what he did next. He faced his clean, shiny window and spit the wreckage onto it! Of course it stuck because of the syrupy candy. The debris was spread over two feet. It was the most disgusting work of art ever created. Black goo with tons of sharp pieces scattered throughout. He then realized that was a wrong move and motioned toward his trash basket. And I just howled and howled. *I know, Mack! I know!*

I kept my job. He never shared my humor in that story, however. When I gave my notice a few years later, Mack also retired. He told me that he'd had the best assistant in me and wasn't interested in training another. Not that I was that trained...

THE PERFECT DAY

O ne year my parents planned a vacation to our Florida home. We were so happy to welcome them to the warmer weather one fall, when things tend to get a little chilly in New England. Our then three-year-old, Becky, was so happy that Grandpa and Grandma were coming to visit.

One morning my father awoke and asked if we wanted to play a game. We were all in. Sure, Grandpa, what will it be? His response was surprising. "How about if we all lived today out as if Jesus Christ were returning to earth today?" Well, that's not the kind of game we have ever played before, but "Sure, let's give it a try," was our response.

Grandma was up first—making breakfast, all cheery and accommodating. Ron decided to vacuum up all the dog hair and debris that usually attached itself to a carpet. *Wow, what helpful family members. I like this game.* After a positive and delicious breakfast, I offered to do the dishes and clean up. Grandma got Becky dressed and cleaned up for the day and straightened up her room as well. We met back in the living room for prayer time, expecting Jesus might pick then to arrive.

31

Prayer time was exceptional: lots and lots of confession and praise time. I mean, if He was coming that day, we were ready.

If someone said something reflecting "the flesh," we would apologize, repent, and move forward immediately. Oh, that thought—sorry, Lord. Oops, should not have raised my voice—sorry, Lord. I should have offered to lift that for her—"Sorry, Lord," became the phrase of the day.

Grandpa thought it would be a good idea to go to the mall to walk, shop, and have lunch. His treat. So, off went the happy, righteous, "perfect" family. No horns beeped on the way or in the parking lot. No money wasted. No one's reaction within the mall's population could get us off course. Not today. Lunch was scrumptious, giving thanks with all five grateful hearts for "our daily bread." The togetherness was so beautiful because it was so perfect. Not one unsolvable problem in the whole afternoon. When someone would make a mistake, it would be readily addressed, forgiveness was quickly achieved, and on we went. Our hearts were pure and loving all day.

When we returned home there were more chores offered and completed. What an efficient little world.

I made dinner. I felt like I should set an extra plate, because I just *knew* Jesus would be there for dinner. But He never showed. Mom cleaned the kitchen. We met for another prayer session after dinner, giving our hearts fully to the Lord and basking in His grace over us. Oh, how blessed we were to be anticipating His soon return. Any minute now.

Even when the sun lowered, I recalled that "every eye will see Him," so I wasn't worried that darkness might hide the cloud He would ride in on.

At about 7:00 PM, Becky was bathed, prayed over, and put to bed. Ah, success. One down, four remained. After more "nice talk" we all decided to go to bed early. After all, we were exhausted. Being perfect is hard work. All were in bed by 7:30 PM. Hugs, kisses, and thank-yous were exchanged. But we had no more "nice" in us. We needed to sleep hard and long after being so "good." The Lord would have to wake us up if he came before midnight. Well, He never showed .

Early the next morning we were all still there. The first sentence out of Grandpa's mouth was, "Hey, wanna play that game again today?" The shouts were loud and in unison: "*Nooooooo!*"

Paul's words to the Galatians say it best: "God saved you through faith as an act of kindness. You had nothing to do with it. Being saved is a gift from God. It's not the result of anything you've done, so no one can brag about it" (Ephesians 2:8, 9).

Again, God's strength over ours. Knowing His grace covers all the ugly areas of sin within me gives me the ability to arise day after day and live life abundantly and for His glory. Resting in His perfection is the best way to live perfectly. Actually, it's the only way.

SMALL MOUTH

We were living in Tampa, and my husband had accepted a position in South Florida. Obviously, the commute was simply too long for Ron to travel daily, so he was invited to stay with my brother for a time. We were thankful we didn't have added expenses, but the difficult truth was that our family was split into two camps. Becky and I quickly devised a plan that would include frequent visits to see her Dad and uncle; we would travel to them. Five hours with a little four-year-old could be challenging, but we would make this work. About an hour into our initial voyage, her mother realized just how long five hours would be. And so "Small Mouth" was born.

I pursed and scrunched my lips into a very small "o" and started talking in a soft, timid-like voice with perfect pronunciation. Becky immediately responded to her "new friend." She asked "her" a variety of questions, including her name and what she liked to do. What an amazing interviewer. Small Mouth had many fears and only one finger (I tell you, I was desperate!). I watched the tenderness of my daughter's heart unfold that day. Small Mouth had a fear of dust and people who treated her unkindly (whoever else lived in her world, I have no idea!). So we talked for quite some time during our journey. There was no script to follow, so things evolved as we cruised the freeway. Oh what fun to live this spontaneous, creative chapter with little Becky.

After I desired my own self back, I was so surprised that Becky then told *me*, her mother, all that had gone on with Small Mouth, citing perfect retention of every fact. So we continued this game in a whole new way. That was good for another fifty miles. Then she shared Small Mouth with other family members, giving credibility to this new solid friendship.

Small Mouth visited us for years, always with that extra step of retelling and further discussion with Mom after "she" left. God helped us get through some difficult circumstances using Small Mouth as a teacher for one great student.

There were silly variations of Small Mouth through the years by some of my siblings... V Mouth (putting two fingers in the shape of a *V* and placing over lips and speaking in *V* words only), and Big Mouth (opening the mouth as wide as it would go and barely communicating). Yes, I come from a long line of loons.

I have to secretly wonder if Small Mouth will ever come to visit Becky's children in the days ahead. Oh, that this grandmother could watch that unfold. Sheer joy would reside in my heart.

THE PLATE

O h, that you could gaze upon this plate. In this case, seeing *is* believing. This original piece of artwork was fashioned by the chubby little hands of a kindergartener named Rebecca. Art class is so much fun for little people. There is no right or wrong; there is just impression, experience, bold ideas and the end product… and it's always a masterpiece.

One afternoon I walked to school to pick up our six-year-old. As we walked home, she told me all about her day, as was our custom. She always had great days. Her cute little personality, bright mind, and readiness for school showed the rest of the world how to live: childlike, brave, equipped, and joyful.

As we arrived home, she reached into her little backpack and handed me all of her daily treasures, giving a full and interesting commentary on each one. That was the first time I saw the plate. It was a white, plastic dinner plate with renderings comprised of black and pink markers. There were three upright stick figures in pink. The first one was smiling. The second was smaller and was smiling. The third matched the size of the first one, but was frowning. At the feet of the family was a horizontal coffin-like black body. A frown was on that face also. There were pink hearts and stars all over. The message on the bottom said, "Love You, Becky." The signature and the heading (in young teacher handwriting) told me we had the right plate: "The Aguiar Family 1987."

I admired her great work, placed it over the kitchen sink, and we went about our afternoon. But the admiration lasted only until her father walked through the front door for dinner that night.

When Ron noticed the new art piece, he took it down and asked Becky all about it. She explained her stick drawings and illustrations with gusto, as any accomplished artist would have done. Dad asked, "Who's this?" as he pointed to the first pink figure. "That's Mommy." she proudly responded. I must say, I looked great as a thin, smiling stick!

Expecting that she would be the smaller, middle person, Ron asked about the second person in the family portrait. Becky enthusiastically responded, "That's the baby." I was pregnant with her brother at the time. We had taught her that a baby is a person even before it is born, so the baby had its own place on the plate. What a pro-life little girl. Pretty neat that he made the plate before he even arrived. A smiling, unborn stick!

When further questioned who the third person with the frown was, Becky simply stated, "That's me."

"Becky, why are you frowning?" he asked. She could not seem to remember.

Oh no! The only other "thing" left on the plate was the black rectangular box with a frown on his face. In a mortified tone, Dad asked, "And who's this?" She proudly replied, "That's Alii." our Dalmatian. Well, she had the black half right.

37

No white to offset his spots, however. That was it: the *whole* family. Ron commended her on her great work, and off she went to ride her bike.

I looked into his grief-stricken face, which clearly relayed the message of his heart: "I didn't make the plate! I am not in her world! The unborn baby and dog made the picture! Where am I?" He placed it back over the sink, but his heart was broken.

Ron has always been the hardest worker, the best husband and father. But working late into the night, as his job required him to do, he was not always home to tuck her in. She didn't know that he was home keeping her safe every night. Many nights he came home after she was sound asleep, would stop in her bedroom, kiss her cheek, caress her face, brush her hair with his hand, and would be out the door before she awoke. That was his sacrifice for us. But in a six-year-old's world, I guess it looked differently. He took a personal inventory that day and reevaluated his priorities. His work habits changed the next day.

At age thirteen, Becky was enrolled in another school; art class now involved brown and pink markers on a ceramic plate, and I am happy to declare the 1994 version of The Aguiar Family had everyone on it. We are all smiling, starting with Dad! The Dalmatian had gone to doggie heaven, and was replaced with our pet beagle. The festive hearts and stars encompassed the happy family, and the message around the rim of the plate said everything Ron needed to hear: "Happy Father's Day! Dad, I love you. Becky"

Oh yes, all was right in the world once again. We have kept both plates through the years, and we have shared them with many who may have needed to hear the lesson we learned so many years ago.

Thank you, Becky, for the great lesson in priorities.

AGA/SGA

After having one child and three miscarriages, we decided to try one more time. Becky was six and an adorable only child. She ruled the roost, and everyone knew it. She loved being around people, was very loquacious, and was a joy to be around. We were living in Florida at the time we received the happy news of this fifth pregnancy. Things were off to a great start, and confidence was building that this baby would make it.

It was now five weeks from the scheduled due date, and we had narrowed the name search to three names. If this child were a little girl, she was to be named Casey Ann. If it were a little boy, his name would be either Andrew Gordon or Scott Gordon. Gordon was selected in honor of my father, and subsequently my brother. Becky was in kindergarten that particular morning, and I had had a time of concentrated prayer about this new little life inside of me. We were not given the luxury of a sonogram, so we had no idea what was coming. A sister for Becky? Or a little brother? I pleaded with the Lord to tell me. I could not wait another five weeks now that we had possible names. "You are knitting this baby together in the secret place, and You know what gender it is. Can't You share this great news with me *now?*" I begged. Yes, I believe prayer should be intensely personal and to the point. Good thing He's not offended by my direct approach. He's bigger than anything I bring to Him. That being said, I heard nothing. I saw nothing. *Get up and get moving, Nancy; your daughter is about to get out of school.* So I did. I walked to school and brought my darling daughter home, listening to every story in her eventful half day.

We had errands to run that afternoon, so after lunch off we went to do some grocery shopping. Becky and I had been working on recognizing and identifying license plates — Florida is the perfect state for learning them. Everyone goes there — people come from all over the USA. As I pulled into the Publix parking lot, my eyes caught a New York plate. The vehicle was a shiny blue and white Lincoln, parked directly in front of us. It was a sign. Instead of quizzing Becky as to where that car was from, I simply shouted, "Becky, you are going to have a brother!"

This is how God relayed that message to me that day: My eyes picked up a different state to get my attention. Then I noticed that this car was blue and white. At precisely the moment it was parked there, there was an open space for me to park directly behind it with no obstruction. Had we been thirty minutes earlier or forty-two minutes later or had parked across the lot, the message would have been lost. This was for *me*! What a blessing to have Him arrange things with such precision and speak so clearly.

The license plate message plainly gifted me that afternoon. No more doubts. God had responded to me through a stranger from New York that day. The plate read: AGA *little Statue of Liberty in the center* SGA. Andrew Gordon Aguiar or Scott Gordon Aguiar. We had the freedom to choose his name, but a boy was coming our way. Don't you love it when God meets you so tenderly? So specifically? So timely? When He stoops to visit our small world in a huge way? It wasn't as much about "the what" as much as it was about "the Who."

The next week some dear neighbors were throwing me a baby shower. The hostess had the conventional blue and pink plastic utensils and a theme that went with either boy or girl. I boldly said, "Cindy, the pink pieces will not be necessary: It's a boy!"

She quickly responded, "You didn't tell me you went to the doctor."

"Well, actually God, who is the Author of Life, told me," I explained. She had no idea how to reply, so she obediently did as she was asked. All blue it shall be .

Five weeks later, I delivered a healthy 8 lb., 12 oz. baby boy; Scott Gordon Aguiar had entered our world! And God has made everything very good.

ONE SUNDAY IN GEORGIA

We were once part of a young but mighty fellowship in Georgia. We didn't have a building to worship in yet, so we rented out a daycare center each week. You may know what that looks like: setting up chairs, rearranging the rooms for kids, staffing rooms for childcare, tearing down all that had been set up—every week. But we were young and committed to serving one another. The preaching was powerful, the people friendly, and it was our second family. And we all had our "regular" seats pretty much every week.

During this period we had a very meager income, as we were a struggling one-income family. We decided that I would be at home with our children (a decision we have never regretted). But all our bills were paid on time, and food was on the table every day. Thanks be to God.

One Sunday—Palm Sunday, to be exact—after all opening activities had been completed, we went to take our seats. I noticed a white envelope with my name on it on "my" chair. I thought, *How fortunate to get mail on Sunday. Such fun.* I opened it up before the service started and found an unbelievable gift.

The unsigned note commissioned me to purchase new Easter dresses for me and my daughter; $75.00 was enclosed. I was stunned! Shocked! Amazed! Waaaaaay more than either of us could ever have imagined spending on new dresses. I immediately spun around to see who might be watching their gift change our lives. But no one gave the secret away. What an unexpected joy, rooted in such lavish generosity, arrived that morning.

You can't imagine how gorgeous we looked on Easter morning. A risen Lord who overcame the grave and His radiant followers worshipping Him in their finery. Years later I understood the grand concept that it is more blessed to give than to receive. But on that occasion I could not imagine anything greater than receiving.

The Lord loves to bless His children by using others. Often the ways for us to truly live more abundantly is by investing generously in those with greater needs than our own.

HURRICANE HUGO

We were living in Charlotte, North Carolina, in a rental home in 1989. Ron was an area consultant with a rather large area of stores to visit at that time. A hurricane warning had been issued; the storm was expected to hit the coast of South Carolina. Although it was listed as a powerful category five in strength, we were a state away and didn't feel too concerned. Ron was on the road, and I was home with our two children. Then the update came: landfall in the Charleston area would be soon, winds were clocked at 160 mph, and things were unraveling quickly. It became apparent that its path would be coming toward Charlotte, where we were. Well, don't hurricanes always weaken when they hit land? I guess not. This thing kept coming, weakening a tad but then re-strengthening. Ron was racing a hurricane to get home. I felt like Dorothy in Kansas as she watched the winds increase while trying to find her family members. Finally I saw that small white Honda approach the driveway, and welcomed my man home with open arms. We put the kids to bed (upstairs), and crawled in bed and waited and waited, living out our faith in the literal dark. We had no electrical power by now. As the wind picked up, my thoughts started to wander, wondering if the roof would hold and why on earth we had put the kids up there. What if our bedroom window broke, shattering glass in our faces? You know those kinds of rogue, uncomfortable thoughts that randomly come? We had our heads under the covers with a flashlight (just in case the glass broke). The old house was rattling now.

Somehow in the midst of 90 mph winds I felt the power and presence of Almighty God. I got out of bed and went to the rattling window and looked into blackness (don't have a clue what I thought I would see). Absolute darkness. I felt like the nation of Israel when the death angel was visiting homes, but God's people were spared because of the blood of the lamb on the doorposts. Yes, it was our own sort of Passover. During the eye of the storm, an eerie sense of stillness came. Finally sleep came. The kids never stirred. What sound sleepers they were.

When we got up the next morning to assess the damage, we found our front step wrought-iron railing in the neighbor's yard and half of the privacy fence down. That was the only damage. Our power was off for three days, but many in our community were without electricity for a full week. Thirty-four lives were lost during that huge storm. We thanked God for His great protection and went to church to worship Him, knowing we had been spared by His mercy.

ONE THANKSGIVING

I don't know if you have ever had a back spasm or not, but they are not fun and can come on very suddenly. One November my back gave way, and I was sentenced to lie in my bed for the typical four days it takes for me to get through it. Day one gave way to day two, which entered day three. Day three was the Wednesday before Thanksgiving. I *needed* to be up and at church by 7:00 PM. But my back would not cooperate. Complaining ramped up at about 4:00 PM; I tried reasoning with God that all He had to do was touch me, and I would be healed, and that church was His idea. The Wednesday before Thanksgiving is my very favorite service of the year. Still, nothing changed. My husband grabbed both kids, gave me a kiss goodbye, and left me at 6:45 PM. *How dare God leave me in this bed!* I was furious.

God interrupted my pity party in His typical grand design; He invited me to a service right there in my bedroom. I resisted it with thoughts like, *There is no piano here. Just You and me? Seriously? Who will preach?* Don't you love it when you catch yourself asking *God* who will preach?

His Spirit prompted me to tell Him something I was thankful for. Reaching down to the lowest common denominator, I answered, "I am alive." His Spirit prompted, *Great! What else?* "I am so thankful for a great husband." He steered me forward, *Yes. Is there anything else?* "I have the two greatest kids in the world." *They are My gift to you. What next?* "I am so thankful you helped through those three miscarriages, although I wish we could have kept them." *Yes, Nancy… continue to tell Me all the things you are thankful for,* He continued.

I took a piece of paper and a pencil from the nightstand and simply put a small upright line on the page as I gave thanks for one thing after another. At the conclusion of our "service" I counted 632 strokes of that pencil! And I put down the pencil, not because I was finished but because I was tired. Oh, Lord, forgive me when I complain and demand my own way! It is not attractive at all, but He is rich in mercy and abounding in love. It truly was the very best service I have ever attended. Just Him and me — perfection.

TWELVE DAYS OF CHRISTMAS

One year, while living in Atlanta, we were in a rough place financially. Christmas was approaching, and very little would be allocated for gifting. We loved the spirit of Christmas on all levels. But this year would be different — or so I thought.

Twelve days before Christmas my husband walked outside to scrape ice off the windshield of our car and found a beautifully wrapped gift with a tag that read, "On the first day of Christmas, someone gave to me one puffy penguin." He brought it inside for us to delight over. We were shocked, amazed, giddy, and grateful.

The next morning I was out of the house first and found *another* brightly wrapped gift with the tagged announcement reading, "On the second day of Christmas someone gave to me two little Muppets." *You are kidding me! Who on earth is doing this?*

And on it went for twelve days, each day increasing the number of gifts that were left for us. Three graduated tins of homemade goodies, four Victorian ornaments, five cans of soda, six candy canes, seven types of cheeses…

These amazing gifts were delivered all different times of the day and night. And we never caught the little elf/elves responsible for blessing us that Christmas. The night before Christmas I wrote a thank you card and stuck it in our wreath that hung on our front door. I sat in the dark of the front room, hoping to catch a glimpse. Nothing. Finally I went to bed at 2:00 AM. We awoke the following morning and found a miniature Christmas tree with twelve McDonald's coupons attached to the branches with clothes pins, and the thank you note was gone. This angel did not want to be known and made that very clear. And throughout the many years that have followed that season, we have thanked and prayed for them. What an incredible gift to us that year was. We, in turn, have paid it forward a number of times.

One year we selected an unhappy neighbor who we hoped could be transformed through some kindness. On the first day of Christmas I tried to recreate the brightly colored wrapping and the same kinds of messages but with different gifts. We came up with presents for our kids as well, so this neighbor would not be too suspicious. We were the only neighbors she would speak with, as she had had a very difficult life and did not trust anyone at all. My husband dodged sunrises, sunsets, and barking dogs, crawling on his belly to avoid being seen by distrustful peeking neighbors to successfully deliver our first gift: a simple box of chocolate-covered cherries. I was so excited for Hilda to be blessed this season.

Four hours after the package was delivered, my phone rang. It was Hilda. "Nancy, I have a bomb in my garage," was all she said in her heavy Austrian accent. What on earth? She said someone had left a bomb on her front doorstep. She must have transported it to her garage. I went over to investigate her claim. "Hilda, the note says 'On the first day of Christmas someone gave to me one box of cherries.' That's it. A gift. Enjoy them." But in her heart everyone was out to harm her; no goodwill was left on earth. I thought to myself that this could be a verrrrrry long twelve days. When we opened the package and found that it was, in fact, an unopened box of candy, she relaxed a bit and accused me of giving it to her. I quickly told her that we had received one basketball from the same anonymous person. Bases covered.

By day three, Hilda was a child anticipating a gift from someone, anyone. She called me at 6:30 AM on day four, asking what we had received. No more sleeping in over Christmas break. But what joy filled our hearts to watch this angry woman soften up and receive gift after gift. On day twelve she received twelve light bulbs, telling her that "Jesus is the Light of the World! Merry Christmas."

THE TREE

In February of 1990 we purchased a beautiful home in the mountains of Asheville, North Carolina. Over forty different types of trees and shrubs landscaped the property. Spring started the process of filling in the bare trees one by one. Come summer, all were dressed with a variety of colors, fragrances, and shapes. Except one. There before us was the naked sixty-foot white oak. In speaking with our new neighbor, he revealed that this once majestic giant had been struck by lightning two years ago. No leaves would ever again grace this enormous skeleton of a tree.

Our friend, Johnny, a lumberjack from Atlanta, made the trip north to give us an estimate of how much it would cost to take this massive skeleton down. He said it would be a three-man job: $500. After just buying this place and all the expenses that go with being a new home owner, it was like a million dollars to us. We decided to put aside two dollar a week until we could afford the project. Ridiculous, I know. But it was a start.

Nine weeks and eighteen dollars into our new plan, I sat down to have lunch in the sunroom, overlooking the tree. As I gave thanks for my meal, I prayed one simple question, "Lord, what are we going to do about that tree?"

Eleven hours later, God mightily answered my question. My husband, Ron, went into the kitchen at approximately 10:30 PM to get a drink of water and heard screeching tires on the back road. Moments later, a man appeared at our front door, telling us that a huge tree had fallen over the road and luckily he had just missed hitting it. Ron immediately called the Fire Department and hurried out to investigate. He rushed back inside to update them. "Please bring your chainsaws. We have a massive tree blocking both lanes on the street."

The firefighters arrived quickly, safety measures were put in place to safeguard others from running into the tree, and the roar of several chainsaws in the dark of night gave the impression that the largest army of termites had arrived to devour that monstrous tree. Music to my ears .

One holy puff from El Shaddai in the quiet of the evening — there was no storm or rain — and our tree was leveled. Had it fallen forward, it would have damaged our house. Had it fallen to our right, it would have destroyed the neighbor's house. But in God's precision and provision, He laid it down (silently!) across the road on undeveloped land under a blanket of darkness, with no witnesses. Sometimes He makes a public display, and the world looks on amazed. And sometimes He likes to work alone, impressing a handful of onlookers. The element of surprise, beholding His awesome power and might, can leave us awestruck.

As I scoped out the aftermath at first light, I realized I was standing on holy ground. A massive, overturned root system lay on the side of the road while many enormous log sections were stacked everywhere at the edge of the property. The scene revealed that the two saplings on either side of this colossal tree were unaffected, and not one link in the chain link fence was crooked. The intricacies of this covert mission were carried out with fine and deliberate detail. Standing amazed, stunned, and humbled, I was reminded of the reaction the disciples had when Jesus calmed the storm. "Who then is this? Even the wind and the sea obey Him!" (Mark 4:41) We were overjoyed by His visit to our home that quiet evening. I cried as I stood there in the backyard. What good fortune.

When I relayed the amazing story to my father the following day, he simply commented, "Nancy, you must have needed something big." I think he was right.

Never underestimate a simple, faith-filled prayer before an Almighty God; He listens to His children. I recalled the prayer I offered the day before: "What are we going to do about that tree?" What on earth was I thinking? I laughed at the pronoun "we." The $18.00 *we* had saved was put it into the offering plate the following Sunday.

SNOW ON THE MOUNTAIN

O ne wintry night, before everyone had a cell phone, Ron was headed home from Louisville to Asheville. A very big and dangerous snowstorm was predicted to hit our area. The kids and I were preparing for Dad's momentary arrival. The clock ticked forward, but no one arrived. We took turns looking out the back window while the snow started slowly falling. Then more rapidly, gravity grabbed heaven's cold precipitation. Our grass was now blanketed white, trees were tall, thin snowmen, and the continual quiet flakes heralded that the storm had officially arrived. Minutes turned into hours.

Oh no, only the moon now governed its dim light, and our house was getting colder and colder. We had lost power. No, it's not summer, and no, we are not living in Florida. This is cold, hilly country, and Daddy is missing.

I thought of building a fire in the main living room. But we could not use the fireplace, as we had it repaired two days before, and the curing needed *three* days. What are the chances of our being in this predicament? Unreal.

I quickly devised a Plan B. The kids and I must gather together in one bed with blankets, comforters, and every other shred of fabric the house had to offer. The temperature was going down very rapidly. I felt like the pea in the 1835 classic story "The Princess and the Pea" by Hans Christian Anderson, under the weight of all the textiles upon me.

Bathroom breaks were freezing and infrequent. Cold hardwood floors and cold toilets—need I say more? It felt as if someone had left the back door wide open. We would retreat back to bed with such efficiency. Every now and then we took turns going to the kitchen (the *long* walk) to get a bite to eat. But all had to be shared among the three of us, and time "in the elements" was not our friend. Everything had to be planned out before the covers swung open to release the next hunter. We took turns—it was the fair thing to do. Usually I tried to make situations into games for the kids, but I didn't think I could sell them on the "freezing to death" game.

Scott sprinted down the long, frigid corridor, turned left into the kitchen, made his selection of what to feed his family, and hightailed it back under the covers. Scott had conquered the task masterfully. As if wearing the Olympic gold medal, this four-year-old presented his mother and sister with dinner: ONE HOTDOG! *Are you serious, son?* We made it last, nibbling every few moments until it was gone. Why on earth don't they make all hotdogs longer so that they match the size of the bun? We sure could have used a longer frank back then.

Every few hours someone would venture a look outside to see if a few black wheels or a bit of chrome on Dad's white car could be spotted. It was just not to be. And the snow kept falling, and I couldn't stop wondering why he hadn't called us. *Lord, watch over all of us,* was my continual cry. I believed wholeheartedly that Ron was in a ditch on the side of some highway, somewhere in that six-hour journey. My thoughts wandered from how hurt was he to how cold was he. Then the all-consuming thought: is he is still alive? This is just not like him at all. He is so responsible. My emotions vacillated between fear and anger all night.

We dozed, awoke, took our quick jaunts, laughed (a little), and endured that terrible night. At first light I checked the driveway. Still nothing. Where on earth was Ron? Why had the phone beside my bed not rung one time?

In assessing the record snowfall, I noticed that a neighbor three houses down the street from us had smoke coming from their *working* chimney. The kids and I wrapped ourselves in our warm parkas and trudged in the deep, new fallen snow to Bob and Betty's house. Invited or not, here we come.

This older couple welcomed their neighbors royally. They shared with us the warm homemade soup and cornbread sitting atop their fireplace insert.

As tough as things were for us that day and night, and going fourteen hours without electricity or heat, Ron was stuck in eighty miles of traffic and spent an entire night on a mountain in his car. No food. No water. No bathroom. No blankets. No one to visit with. No phone. The state police closed the road with those cars on it until it was safe to open. When we finally saw that white Honda drive up the back driveway, we were so overjoyed!

Hardship is the class no one signs up for. But there are benefits involved: patience is built, staying power is developed, perseverance is applied, stamina is stretched, and fortitude is established. Yes, we are better for having been through such adversity.

57

BANANA BREAD

One Saturday morning I was awakened earlier than usual with a prompting to make a loaf of banana bread. I fought the desire to leave the comfort of my warm bed, but God seemed insistent that I get moving. I gave every flimsy excuse, but eventually I found myself marching toward the kitchen. I wondered if I even had all of the ingredients that the recipe required. Just then I turned to enter the kitchen, only to find three overripe bananas. Don't you hate it when God always thinks ahead and you just have to obey? I began to blend the ingredients, thankful for a mostly quiet house, and put this little gem into the oven to bake. Then the Lord gave the next directive: *I want you to bring it to Betty.* Betty is an older woman who lives two doors down from us. What? I was perplexed, needless to say. The homemade smell was now reaching the nose of my husband and the bedrooms of our children, who were excited at the prospect of some fresh bread. Nope, not for you guys—sorry.

After the loaf had cooled, I wrapped it up, changed my clothes, and walked across the street to Bob and Betty's house. I thought, *Early on a lazy Saturday morning? This must be some sort of crime. No one wants to see me at this hour. And I certainly don't want to be visiting anyone at this hour either.* Oh, does our flesh get in the way sometimes. As I approached their front door, rang the doorbell, and looked into the eyes of my neighbor, the Lord finally told me the rest of the story. I now fully understood what He was up to that morning. My first words to her were, "This is the day, isn't it?" Through tears, she said, "Yes, it is."

Bob and Betty had lost their twenty-nine-year-old son ten years ago to the day in a fatal car accident. We hugged and wailed as only two mothers could that morning. I had never met their son, as we had moved into the neighborhood after he had died. We talked of what the day would hold for her and her husband. Such sadness, such loss, such pain filled that day. As we sat at her kitchen table that morning, she entrusted to me all I had missed in not knowing her young son. She shared many fond memories of him. How Robby came to life through his mother's voice.

As we parted ways that morning, I envisioned the older couple exchanging their bathrobes for proper attire, probably speaking little, crying frequent tears throughout the day, and making the somber trip to their son's grave — a destination no parent wants to visit. As I reflected on our short visit, it became apparent to me that a gift had been given and one was received.

Betty was overjoyed that I had remembered her on that dreadful day. I told her it was God who remembered and He was just using a neighbor to show His deep love for her. Oh, what if I had stayed in bed? God is always working on much deeper levels. I just need to keep paying attention.

TITHING

Don't you just love the greatness of God? I am talking about the times when He can see all angles of everything, and we have only a very limited view of things. I cannot fathom that He sees the entire world from beginning to end at the same time, yet His eye catches a sparrow that falls to the ground. Simply astounding.

So why do we doubt when we *know* this? My only explanation is that we are limited to our humanness, and He is not. And when He teaches these lessons, you just don't seem to forget them. This one particular time God impressed such a lesson upon me.

My family had an unusually large number of expenses that more than devoured our bi-weekly paycheck. I watched for Him to make His move to allow us to make ends meet that pay period. As I handle our finances, I felt solely responsible and didn't want to share this bad news with my husband. No, I would take this to God, our Provider, and Him alone. Why do we sometimes desire to take full responsibility for things? It seemed as though this was my fault. Why couldn't I manage things better? I pleaded with God to bail us out, but no miracle appeared. Monday quickly became Tuesday. Nothing. Tuesday turned into Wednesday. Nothing changed. Wednesday is gone in a flash. Zilch. I was desperate for something. Anything.

Payday was not until next Friday, and I was writing checks here and there throughout the week, believing in my unseen, quiet God. "Lord, it's Thursday. Where are You?" I lament. Silence.

I came to that moment of decision on Saturday, being tempted by You-Know-Who. To write our tithe check or not... that is the question. I had every reason by human standards to forego a "nonessential" check. "God, we are in dire straits here," I whined. "Our church will get by this week without our little check, I'm sure. Lots of people will be giving You Your due this weekend. Can we have a pass this week? Please?"

Don't you sheepishly cower when you replay these kinds of conversations with the Master of the Universe in your head? I thought, *Maybe it's time to test Him with the impossible. That prophet of old, Malachi, instructs and invites us to test God in a matter like this — well, there's no time like now to test Him.* Crazy, I know, but I decided to write the full tithe check, praying for Him to provide the funds to cover it.

Ron dropped the little envelope in the offering plate that Sunday, and I found myself desperate for God to once again provide. Surely He would bring His provision on Monday. That was the drop dead last day He must provide. Otherwise we would be overdrawn in about four states — and our own church.

I kept watch over the door to our house, the wall phone, and the mailbox, anxiously awaiting my answer, but there was no knock, no call. It had to be in the mail then. I walked slowly, very slowly, to my last hope—the little gray metal box at the end of our driveway. "God, I need a ram in the thicket," I solemnly prayed. Abraham got that because he believed. "I have put everything on Your Name here. Help my unbelief."

As if waiting for an acceptance letter, I gingerly opened the flap only to find no mail. *Oh, my. This is the only day of my life there has been nothing in the mailbox. Nothing. Not even an advertisement?*

In my shock and horror, I remembered it was a national holiday: Martin Luther King, Jr. Day. I've never been so thankful for that man's contribution to our world—or that it earned him a day off from postal delivery and banking. *Breathe, Nancy. Praise your Father for His gracious gift!*

God's providential hand was seen at the end of the driveway that day; there was a ram in my thicket. My spirit skipped all the way back to the house. Tomorrow is not here yet. Today is covered. I was free to worship and live another day. I even thought of praying like Joshua, asking for the sun to stay still and not to let there be a Tuesday.

Angst returned twenty-four hours later. Although the day before had been its own sort of miracle, I was not aware of any holiday falling on the Tuesday following MLK, Jr. Day. My Father would take charge of this day, too. But it would defy all human logic.

On Tuesday I reached into the letterbox and pulled out several pieces that could not hold my interest. Then I saw a familiar return address from an angel of sorts who lived a few states away. As I opened the thin envelope my eyes watered as I gazed upon a personal check for $1,000. There was no way to justify this gift! A bolt out of the blue! The note attached gave me the freedom to "use as you see fit."

Right then and there, I dropped to my knees and worshipped Almighty God. I stayed on my knees for approximately twenty minutes, thanking God for His faithfulness, love, timing, provision and for the obedience of others to listen and obey Him as He instructs. What a lasting memory.

As I promptly drove to the bank, I decided not to speed, as I would not have had the extra money to pay the ticket, and I would not ask Him for more grace.

God says, "Test Me. Trust Me. Turn to Me." He urges us to come so He can turn our trials to triumph. It's what He does. Only God.

THE WEDDING/THE RENEWAL

My first marriage ceremony took place in Las Vegas in the same chapel where Elvis was married. Both Ron and I were unsaved at the time, so we didn't fully understand what marriage meant on a spiritual level. We had a fifteen-minute ceremony, officiated by a stranger who seemed like a used car salesman in short sleeves, but that was okay. Mom, Dad, two of my sisters and my brother-in-law were in attendance. Oh yes, and God was also there, because He is Omnipresent. The record player was initiated, playing "Here Comes the Bride." My father walked me down the aisle, a full six paces, to the front of the chapel, where Ron was waiting for me. You know when you are just so in love that nothing around you matters but that man in front of you? Dad had purchased the deluxe wedding package, which included ten large photographs of us in a white album. The year was 1977. We were living high.

One of the reasons Las Vegas was chosen was that it was a fun city in the middle of our two homes, Massachusetts and Hawaii. We planned it so both families could attend with only half the distance to travel, but Ron's father was ill and unable to make the trip. His mother stayed with his father, so my family members were the only ones who attended, after all.

How we have laughed about that ceremony throughout the years. And to think of the other Vegas options we could have selected brings forth even more laughter. Another chapel we visited was a very popular place, but as we entered, we saw a man boxing with a kangaroo wearing boxing gloves, and Ron said there was no way he could tell his grandchildren that we had gotten married with a fighting kangaroo in attendance. The marsupial was much faster than the man, and I just knew the man was going down soon. We have never regretted the decision not to marry there.

After nineteen years of marriage, Ron did the unthinkable. It was Christmas Eve, 1996, and all of our family was in on the surprise but me. Ron handed me a slender 5" x 7" envelope at the very end of the evening, as our excited kids looked on. I opened it and started to cry. He gave me an invitation to my very own church wedding! Yes! We would renew our vows in a Bible-based, Christian church. He had selected a wedding coordinator, singers, and our preacher... and the date would be four days after our twentieth anniversary. We had nine months to plan our wedding renewal.

We invited friends and family, and they came from eight states. New dresses and suits were purchased, friends helped with music, food, decorating the fellowship hall, serving our guests, and cleaning up. I felt like a twenty-four-year-old bride again.

I asked my coordinator if my father was to walk me down the aisle again. She kindly said, "No, he already has. You and your husband walk down the aisle together, as you are already married." Duh! I tell you, I have never done this before.

What a special ceremony it was. On September 20, 1997, we renewed our vows before God, family, and friends.

I really loved both of my ceremonies because they showed the contrast of where we were then and where we were twenty years in. A significant shift in our maturity and thinking had, in fact, been realized. Praises to our patient, merciful, and saving God.

But the best gift of that great and glorious day came at 10:30 PM that evening. High heels had been kicked off, and family was gathered around as we relived the wonderful event that had taken place earlier that day. A precious few were remembering back to Las Vegas twenty years ago when the phone rang. At 10:30 PM? *Who on earth could that be?* I answered it, and heard a familiar voice on the other end of the line: my old boss from the days of working for Coca-Cola in Atlanta. He didn't even know of our celebration that day. Just a random day, time, and call, almost as if God waited for all the festivities to cease and carefully placed one more gift before us.

Mack. It was so great to hear his voice. He proceeded to tell me the greatest news. After seventeen years of praying for this dear man, he had finally surrendered his life to Jesus. God had intercepted him from a planned suicide. He filled me in on every detail and ended with "I thought you would want to know." Um, *yes*! I told him what a day of celebration it had been, but that his call was my greatest gift of the entire day. Now mind you, the only way I had ever heard him speak of Jesus was in a profane way. Here he was praising that name!

Wow—what a shift in his perspective of Him. It was music to my ears. We talked about his final destination quite a bit, as he was in failing health. But we both rejoiced in his excellent decision.

Three months later Mack met Jesus and now lives with Him forevermore in Heaven. It is by God's grace we have been saved, through faith. Not by our own works. Mack met Messiah's miraculous magnetic mercy—magnificent!

Yes, September 20, 1997, was a dazzling and delightful day.

KING'S ISLAND

One year our family was unable to take our annual summer vacation. We always enjoyed being together and getting away, but schedules and finances prohibited it that particular year. A very good friend of ours gave us four tickets to a marvelous theme park, which was located approximately two hours away. But there was one condition: the passes had to be used by the end of October, and we were closing in on the end of the season. Planning was fast and fun; we decided to go the very last day the park was open for the season. All systems were a go, and we were so excited for this one free twenty-four-hour vacation day.

Unfortunately, the weather report was disastrous: 100 percent chance of snow. We did not want to hear that report, with no time left to change the date and two excited kids squeezing a week of vacation into one day. Two dubious parents made a hotel reservation, loaded up the car, and headed north—just *knowing* it was going to be a disaster. We drove through storm clouds as black as night; all our human reasoning screamed, "Don't be so foolish. Stay home. Handle the disappointment here, not there."

Our secondary option was to check into the hotel, have dinner, and shop at a local mall and take in a movie the following day. Ron and I were fully convinced we would be going with Plan B.

But our little first grader made us try to get to the theme park; he was so convinced he would be riding rides all day, and there was no dissuading him. So, off we went, disregarding all logic. We closely watched the storm clouds expand throughout the entire sky and measured the increasingly cooler temperatures as we began our journey. I didn't realize until that day that black can get blacker. The threatening clouds owned the whole sky and were multiplying. More and more black clouds snowballed on the other side of the windshield. I've never seen anything like it.

Before bedding down for the night in our hotel room, I knelt beside my young son's bed, and we went before the Almighty King in prayer as we did every night. How on earth could I be truthful before God and pray for the impossible? My son would have a much greater faith than I that night. I prayed some sort of "vanilla prayer," trusting more in a weather report than in my Creator. I sheepishly asked that God might give us a "good day," a "day of good companionship," a "day of provision in however He saw fit." Scott grabbed the bottom of my blouse and interjected, "Mom, don't forget to ask for good weather, no snow or rain, and the park to be opened." Yikes! That is waaaaaay too daring for me, but I proceeded. "Lord, if You choose, please consider giving us no snow or rain and just maybe a glimpse or two of the sun if that is Your plan for us tomorrow." That was as bold as I could ever utter a request, believing none of it would come to pass. Praying, yet not believing, is a shameful place to be.

As we awoke the next morning, the clouds were even blacker and the weather was colder, but Plan B was never an option for Scott. He would not hear of the possibility of altering our plans from a theme park to a mall. So we bundled up, headed for the car, and drove to King's Island, fully expecting some kind of precipitation to fall. But nothing came. There were no cars in the entire parking lot. We parked in the first space, right by the entrance. Well honestly, who would be there but us? My husband and I were amazed nothing had yet fallen from the skies yet—utterly amazed. So, we headed for the entrance, ready to turn back with every step forward.

We enjoyed the park the whole day with a total of about thirty-five other people. Scott had the day of a lifetime, as there was absolutely no waiting for any ride. Favorite rides were ridden over and over. I traveled the entire park the entire day with my cumbersome umbrella tucked under my arm and never opened it. Not once. Oh, and the sun even peeked out twice. We had the most wonderful vacation that day, as we were so aware that our loving God was with us every step of the way. Just so very thankful.

I think Scott's faith carried the family that day .

THE LAUNDROMAT

Have you ever done something or gone somewhere without knowing why? One morning I just knew I was supposed to go to the laundromat. The problem was that I didn't need to go. My laundry was clean, and my washer and dryer were in working condition. Then why the trip?

The nudge to go was so strong that I had to pay attention to it and go. If I wanted peace, that is. Looking for something to wash, I decided I could wash our king-sized comforter in a commercial washer, as it doesn't fit very well in my standard-sized washer. Bingo. I was finding more peace by the moment.

I seized our monstrous winter comforter and grabbed my purse, car keys, and Bible study. I figured I would be productive while waiting for my assignment to play out. Remembering how expensive laundromats could be, I grabbed about $20 of coins, and off I went.

Upon arrival, I found an open gigantic model that dwarfed my oversized quilt. Perfection. I quickly proceeded to load up the machine with my precious silver.

With step one complete, I started to stroll around the building, seeking an answer for why I was there. Who was my contact? I spotted an older grandmother with her five grand-kids, doing her washing for the week. I made my way over to her. In trying to start a conversation, her body language clearly stated she was task-focused and didn't want any small talk. *Okay, got it.*

I then moved over to another part of the workplace to find a Hispanic gal. "*Hola,*" I offered. Nothing much there beyond the cursory, "*Como estas*?" No one else was around for me to chat with, so I sat down to work on my Bible study homework.

As soon as I opened my workbook and Bible to begin the day's lesson, I heard a clear, sweet voice from four feet above where I was seated. She inquired, "What are you doing?" *Ah, there you are,* I thought to myself. As I turned my head to see who was greeting me, I saw a middle-aged employee perched in a high walled-off seat, like that of a judge in a courtroom. I stood to recognize her and engage in conversation. "I am working on my Bible study while I wait for my comforter to be cleaned," I responded.

She asked more and more questions about the study. She seemed genuinely interested in hearing about it. I shared a few concepts like grace, salvation, and eternal life. Like water on parched land, the truths she'd been searching for filled the cracks and addressed her broken places. It seemed as though she was unchurched at the time and longed for the connection with God and other students of the Word. We had a hearty lesson in the laundromat that day.

My time came to a close there when my bed covering was washed, dried, and folded, and I was ready to exit the warm establishment. I had spent the last two hours sitting and chatting with Sue. We were both sad to leave that stimulating conversation, but daylight was burning. She said, "Nancy, when will you be back again?" How should I answer that? It wasn't exactly my idea to come that day. But that might not sound right, so I simply stated, "I'm not sure…" I popped back in to check on Sue about six months later, as I was wondering how she was doing. She no longer worked there.

God's timing is golden. His ways are not the same as ours; they are so much higher. Consider where He could use you today — oh, and don't forget the quarters if you are selected to visit a laundromat.

ATTITUDE

Every year Ron and I have (at least) one grand evening out when we celebrate our anniversary. We pick a different restaurant every year; no repeats are allowed. We always dressed up and headed out without our children. As there is a span of six and a half years between our youngsters, Becky was always put in charge of her younger brother on this particular evening, and she wasn't always wild about having the added responsibility.

Our seventeenth anniversary arrived. Becky was only thirteen and was put in charge of Scott for several hours. Now, you know how sometimes a sour attitude can spoil your elaborate plans, right? I was bound and determined *nothing* was going to rain on our parade that night.

We were in our bedroom, dressing for our big night out, anticipating the fun, food, fellowship, and fascinating finery that would soon be ours. We finally emerged, ready to leave the kids behind.

I asked Becky for one more favor: would she please take a picture of Dad and me? She, with the attitude of a typical self-centered young teen grabbed the camera while frowning, rolling her eyes, sighing and showing her displeasure with exaggerated drama. Nope, sweetie, you are not going to ruin my night!

Trying to keep the mood light, I asked her, "So, how do you think we look?" She looked at us with a disgusted look and said, "Well, I'm glad your identity is in Christ." *Whaaaaat?* What was supposed to be a hurtful response turned out to be one of my proudest moments in motherhood. Why, Becky, that's one of the greatest things anyone has ever said to me!

Thank you, Becky, for being the added blessing to us that evening so many years ago and for being such a great big sister to your little brother.

BLIZZARD RIVER

Anumber of years ago, my sisters and their families and me and my family signed on for an adventure at Six Flags over New England. Because we usually live our lives separated by a thousand miles, we were overjoyed to have this special occasion. The kids rapidly banded together and ran here and there, discovering new rides to try. We sisters stayed close by and exchanged the many missing components of our different worlds. Ever light-hearted and laughing, we are so different and yet so much the same. Oh, the joys of rich sibling relationships.

Then we saw the ride all six of us would ride: Blizzard River—a round raft-like ride amid the rapids. We patiently waited for our turn to board. Finally we took six of the eight seats offered on our raft. As everyone was belting in before hitting what looked like level four rapids, I found that my belt was not long enough. Oh no—was I going to be denied this fabulous ride? Just then, the diminutive Asian girl working the ride came over to make sure all safety regulations were being enforced. She saw the rogue rider, smiled, and grabbed both sides of my belt to be joined together and tried to force them to engage with the strength of Arnold Schwarzenegger. But to no avail. She then looked me squarely in the eyes, sweetly said in her accented voice, "I am so sorry," and grabbed that severed belt and *made it happen*! No one was more shocked than I was. Where on earth did that strength come from? You have heard of people lifting cars when it was humanly impossible, right? She was a candidate for that, I tell you. I immediately defaulted to laughter. I'm talking hyena-type laughing. Uncontrollably! All six of us were howling. There was no getting me out of that seat; should the ride malfunction, I would be going down with the ship. Waiting for the next three minutes for the ride to start, the six of us howled, laughed, and wheezed. Funniest incident ever! Then I looked at the other two "lucky" passengers traveling with us. They didn't know if they should join us in laughing or not. Their hesitation made me laugh all the harder. Clearly they can observe that I am not offended. I am having the ride of a lifetime. How on earth could they not join in this contagious amusement? Laughter is such good medicine.

I am happy to report that at the conclusion of the ride I tried to release the belt, and just like opening a rolled canister of Pillsbury rolls by pressing the indented line under the wrapper, *Poof!*, I was free.

INTERNATIONAL GUESTS

How can you travel the world and stay put at the same time? By bringing the world to you. If you take a look around, foreigners may be in your midst. In our city, we have residents from Somalia, Bosnia, Cuba, Iraq, Vietnam, Sudan, Liberia, Iran, Congo, Kosovo, and former Soviet Republics, to name a few; believe me, I've taught some of them.

Our family decided to be a host family to a number of internationals along life's pathway. We had Kazuko from Japan as our first student. Her family was so far away in Yokohama that it only made sense for her to come and stay with us while she was in college. You know that house that you needed when the dorm life was a little too much? She was a darling young lady who handsomely cut our hair out of gratitude for what we extended to her. Ron thought that was the greatest gift ever, as he needs a haircut every three weeks. We enjoyed her company for two years until we moved away.

When Kazuko's mother made her maiden voyage to North America to see her beloved daughter, they wasted no time in securing a vehicle and traveled three hours to where we then lived so Mrs. K could give us thanks for showing such kindness to her daughter. Both she and I were reduced to tears on our walkway as our young translator verbalized her mother's heart to her host mother. And as Kazuko spoke her flawless English, her diminutive mother bowed low in Japanese-style respect. What do you do with that? I was given more than my heart could hold.

Alexander, from Siberia, graced our home for two weeks when he was invited to the USA to learn all he could about accounting. He was so interested in everything American. He and Ron stayed up nights beyond 2:00 AM exchanging information. He gave us glimpses of his homeland, his grand-mother's stifled faith (under Stalin's regime), and watched an older Promise Keepers' video in disbelief. There was no way for him to fathom 70,000 men together praising God . He was highly intelligent and darling to know. One night he inquired of us, "How much does the government pay you to house me?" We looked at one another and laughed. "Pay? Um, nothing." Shock spread across his handsome face. "We are led to believe Americans do everything for a price." was his response.

In Alexander's part of the world the pollution was horrible and the air was filthy, so he had a very hard time believing people walked in their houses here with shoes on until he arrived. In his hometown, shoes left on his feet would track in dirt that would trash the rugs immediately. He saw how clean our air was and finally understood. He watched as my husband left for the office in a white shirt. He fully expected to have the seatbelt preserve the only white on his shirt when he returned for dinner. No, if Ron did not spill his barbeque sauce on his shirt during lunch, he would return with it still white.

How amusing discussions are with people who live differently than we do. So much to learn from one another.

We had the pleasure of hosting Vadim, from Moldova, also. He was a natural comedian (and a pharmacist). A gem of a gentleman indeed.

As we hosted these treasured guests, the only request we made of them was that they attended church with us on Sunday morning. And all of them were so willing, as they were brilliant students of life. Their eagerness was so refreshing. We also made each of them a welcome basket and placed it in their room. There was always a New Testament in their heart language, showing them the Way.

I remember passing by Vadim's room one afternoon and saw him propped up on his bed with that little Moldavian Bible opened, filling him with truth. That memory still warms my heart. I am thankful for the Gideons, who provided us with copies every time we needed them.

Vadim truly loved to eat. Everything. He and Scott would sit at the breakfast table with their cereal bowls and compete in silence, seeing who could eat more. Scott's family nickname was "Silo" because he stored grain, lots of it. When Vadim came to the table, he decided to match and even exceed Scott's two bowls of cereal by having three. When Scott realized he'd been outdone, he began having three or maybe even four bowls. Then Vadim upped his portion to five servings of assorted cereals. And on it went .

I started to realize how rapidly we were going through large boxes of cereal. So, I doubled the amount of boxes I bought each week. Was I now contributing to this competition?

I guess in some ways I was. There was that one day that I glanced at thirteen boxes of cereal on the kitchen counter and knew I needed to get to the store quickly, as we were running low. No words were ever exchanged, but everyone was keenly aware of the unnamed contest going on before our very eyes. Hysterical. We still talk about that amusing breakfast battle.

After church one day, we made plans to cross the Ohio River and dine at a great little place where our friend Chef Bob was working. We invited some friends, and sixteen people ended up coming. Yes, lots of people wanted to join us and get to know our new friend a little more. The buffet was elegant, opulent, and opened to the hungriest of worshippers. Our party made a beeline for the homemade waffles and bacon shortly after our prayer of thanks had been offered.

As we ate, we introduced one another and explained to Vadim that all was open and available for him to enjoy as he desired. We laughed, talked, and commented on the excellent quality of our belated breakfast. About an hour into our experience, Vadim quietly addressed me: "Nancy." The hush of the table was deafening, as we loved his questions, interactions, and observations. "Yes, Vadim. What's up?" In all seriousness he asked a question that he genuinely wanted answered, "Can you die from eating too much?"

This innocent lamb was trying to keep up with the Americans and was beyond uncomfortable. Free food? As much as you could eat? Seriously? He'd kept going back over and over and over once he found out it was okay to eat as much as you could. It was estimated he made at least eight trips to the smorgasbord that day and lived to tell the tale.

Alex was our guest for a few days, while my sister (his original host family) had gone on a business trip. He had been a KGB agent in the former USSR. He spoke no English, so we were very limited in our conversations. The great news was that our church's Passion play was going on while he was staying with us, so we were able to secure a ticket for him. I trusted God would lead Alex through the evening, as only He can.

Alex was glued to every movement on the platform that year, thirty rows in front of him. He never took his eyes off the production. The colors, the costumes, the characters, the music — all designed to bring the viewer closer to the Savior of the world, Jesus.

Two hours later, Alex stood with tears in his blue eyes and made motions by clasping his hands to his heart and bringing them outward. The story and sacrifice of Jesus profoundly affected him at the deepest level. It was as if his heart was beating outside of his chest. We were astounded that he got the entire message without the benefit of words.

Later in the week when my sister returned from her trip, we went to her house to drop off Alex. Carole, who speaks Russian well, translated the blessing he bestowed upon our son, Scott. He cupped his hands around the beautiful face of our precious eight-year-old and spoke life over him. Carole translated his profound words directly into our hearts. What an expansive tender heart he had. Now it was our turn to cry.

And of course there were several other guests we grew to know and love: Yuri, Petra, Ion, Tongtong, Ilya, Stefan, and more. About twenty-five to thirty international guests have called our home theirs.

We currently have Eric and Adjoa, from Ghana, who are working hard to achieve doctorates. One will complete the task in four years, and the other will need five. We were overjoyed when Eric decided to be baptized at our church in 2013. Both students have a saving relationship with Jesus. For that, we are very thankful. We were able to plan a party for Adjoa before she flew back home to marry her sweetheart, Idrisu. A few generous friends came over and showered her with gifts, friendship, kindness, and prayers.

Every one of these guests has blessed our lives in numerous ways. We are so very grateful for the chance to have met all of them and know God's plan and purpose has been accomplished.

I cannot wait for our universal Heavenly language one day! A perfect place with no more barriers. I hope to see all of our guests there.

THE BRIDE OF CHRIST

S everal years ago I was asked to speak at a ladies' event out of town. It was to have the theme "The Bride of Christ" and would be held on a Saturday morning at 8:30 AM. The planning committee decided to have wedding dresses and wedding cakes on display and would be serving a buffet breakfast. It was a beautiful idea and caused me to yearn for the marriage feast that would be taking place one day with our Bridegroom, Jesus.

As I began preparing for my talk, I researched Scriptures and added my usual silly stories to drive home certain points and found myself praying for this event over and over again, but it was the persecution I felt throughout the process that startled me. Never had I had such a spiritual struggle preparing a talk as I did during this particular experience. I was working ten times harder and found frustration after frustration as I slowly proceeded. It was unbearable at times.

The enemy of our souls was throwing everything he had at me to frustrate my attempts at delivering a message to the ladies I would meet in the weeks ahead. Yet perseverance was provided by God's powerful Spirit. Triumph came. The talk was completed, and I was ready to present it.

The day arrived, and I seriously thought of wearing the wedding-like dress I wore to my wedding renewal ceremony. Thankfully, at the last minute I changed my mind. I grabbed the directions to the church and headed out. I was driving, singing, praying, and overjoyed that "it was well with my soul."

After an extended time of not paying attention to the directions, I realized the intersection I was looking for was waaaaaaay off. Hadn't the leg that was supposed to be thirty miles felt a little too long? *Surely this cannot be right. I am in farmers' country out here. I have lost civilization. What on earth?* As I reviewed the directions I was given, I realized one of the left/right decisions was very, very vague—maybe I was going in the directly opposite direction of the church. Oh no. Minutes were ticking on the clock, and I began to have severe doubts.

I had to ask someone. Anyone. Not a single soul was out on this particular Saturday morning. *Where on earth are some humans?* I began to speed on the long, vacant country roads. Even the cattle were staring at me, wondering what the hurry was. *Shouldn't farmers be milking cows or something? A mailman? A police officer? A thief?* Finally, after an additional twenty miles or so, there was one mechanic with his bay door open. I screeched down the driveway and politely asked the gentleman where I was. He told me the name of his town, which didn't sound even remotely familiar. I told him where I was headed and asked him to point me there. He chuckled and said, "Oh, that's an hour and a half in the other direction!" I could not believe my ears. I was ninety miles off course? By my clock, only twenty minutes remained until the breakfast began. Panic hit. I am the speaker. I had to call the church and let them know I was coming, but to start without me. *Or should we all just go home? It would be like a bride-to-be jilted at the altar – no, that isn't at all what Jesus would do.* And so my car turned in the corrected direction and continued toward the Marriage Breakfast.

I was speeding at an unsafe pace, praying that no rabbits tried to cross the windy roads. *Man, am I ever out of control! Reckless is more like it. I have never been so embarrassed. These darling leaders have commissioned me to come and encourage their ladies and I don't show?* This was in the days before I had a mobile phone, so there was no calling the church from the car. I begin to look for a pay phone to advise them of my delay. Miles later a convenience shop came into view. I dialed the church's number. Of course no one answered. *They are all in the fellowship hall, fellowshipping. Why would anyone answer my phone call?* I left a message, knowing no one would check it. On the road again, flying mile by mile in the amended direction, I pictured the ladies who had gathered together that morning for a blessing. One questions the other, "So where did you get this speaker again? Does anyone even know her? Has anyone ever even heard her? What are we supposed to do now? Anyone have a word for us if she's a no show? Did we pay her already?" My thoughts were keeping up with the excessive miles per hour my car was going.

It was about then that I heard the officer's siren. *You are kidding me, God! Another delay!* (This was the point I was glad I was not wearing a wedding dress.) The policeman *slowly* approached my door. Isn't everything in slow motion when you are in a rush? Well, this law enforcer was knocking on my window. He asked me my name, and I burst into tears. *I'm ashamed to tell you. My name is MUD in this town. Just call me Mrs. Mud. That will work.* He asked for me to present my proof of insurance. I could find my wallet, but that was it. I was under such stress that I lost my mind; I had no idea where my card was. Which side, which pocket, zippered or not—I hadn't a clue. Amazing what stress does to our systems. He took my license and checked to see what kind of medication the doctor had prescribed, me thinks. I told him my story. I'm sure he'd heard a lot of excuses in his day, but a lady late for her own sermon was probably a new one. He said, "Ma'am, I clocked you at 17 mph over the speed limit. I believe you are trying to do the right thing. Therefore, I am going to waive the trip back to court, but you will be paying a hefty fine for driving so recklessly. I will escort you to the road you need to get to so you can complete your journey."

"Thank you, officer. One hundred percent my fault. One hundred percent my dues to pay."

As I finally approached the church, I entered the driveway excitedly and fishtailed (did not mean to— too much adrenaline.) beyond the pavement and onto the gravel. Finding one open space, I proceeded to grab my things and exit the vehicle. I doubt I could have walked a straight line at that point. Some gentlemen (or angels) met me and asked if I was the speaker. I sheepishly told them I was. They put their arms around my shoulder and prayed the most calming prayer. With God's precision, the words landed in my heart. *Now* I was ready to enter the church.

Upon entering, I was quickly ushered to the stage to begin my talk. My arrival was approximately ninety minutes late, but almost every lady had remained to hear the whole message. As I observed all the emptied dishes in the buffet line, I offered a prayer to our Groom and spoke His words of love, acceptance, and hope.

The amount of adversity I faced during that complete journey tried to hold me captive, but Jesus came to set the captives free. The honorarium was signed over to the courthouse, and life moved forward. A few months later I received a phone call from the Director of Women's Ministry, asking if I could do a retreat for the ladies. They actually wanted me back! I quipped, "Well, if I leave now, I can make it." Unfortunately, I was already booked for the weekend they needed someone. But the forgiving action made its mark on me from those darling, gracious, kind ladies. I am forever indebted.

MY SOLDIER

O ur church used to produce the most amazing pageant of the life of Christ. Every year, church members would sign up to serve in a variety of ways, and auditions for an assortment of parts were conducted. This was an enormous commitment to undertake, as rehearsals were frequent and demands for excellence set the bar high. Serving in this area was not for the faint of heart. School children must pledge to take on their roles in addition to their primary role of students with homework each day, while the older working folks agreed to add about five to six hours to their already full days. Such was life for several weeks for the one thousand brave souls who made that incredible story come alive.

One year I worked on preparing food for one particular group of performers, so I had a little more freedom to come and go. Becky was attending a college out of town, so she was not participating that year. After playing the part of Malchus, the high priest's assistant, the year before, Scott elected to play the part of a Roman soldier that year. And of course Ron had his long, steady shift, balancing his regular job by day and being a nightly watchman in the House of God for this grand total of almost 9,000 guests, the size of a small town, for seventeen nights.

After picking up Scott from school, I dropped him off at church into the capable hands of makeup artists, who were adept at darkening all parts of his body that were not covered with clothing. He very much enjoyed the community of caring, talented people every day.

Our dear friend Jefferson was playing the lead role of Jesus, as he had for several years. Jefferson is an incredibly accomplished actor who memorizes Scripture avidly, loves people as Jesus would have, and gave his all at every presentation. I once heard a lady in the balcony shout "Now *that's* my Jesus!" with all sincerity. Yes, Jefferson made Jesus real, and God's Spirit made sure he kept things accurate and awe-inspiring throughout each practice and performance.

During one particular dress rehearsal that called for the soldiers to be on the platform, something changed within our son, something personal. As "Christ" was placed on the horizontal cross to be nailed to it, someone realized that a soldier was missing from his post right at the crossbeam. Scott was asked to stand in for him. He took his place, trying to be the hard-hearted, unsympathetic, calloused Roman guard he was trained to play. Just then the flogged, beaten, bloodied Jefferson made eye contact with him. Eyes of love. Wracked with pain. Darkness reigning for a brief period. And the blood of "Jesus" splattered on our son. How personal the story had just gotten for Scott. How affected was this young actor. How like Jesus to bring us into His story. He came to cover us in His precious blood.

When I picked up my son from practice that evening, he started the story by saying, "Mom, I got Jesus' blood on me tonight!" Well, of course, son .

Thank you for making it personal, Jefferson. And for making it *real*, Jesus.

ALASKA

I was invited to participate in my first mission trip in the fall of 2002. Ten ladies were traveling to Alaska for ten days for a Christian conference. We were all to speak or sing, present a visual form of our testimonies to the churches, and facilitate small groups as they had need. My traveling team was extraordinary, and the ladies from the churches we worked with in Alaska were amazing.

My very dear and thoughtful daughter, Becky, had written ten encouraging cards for me to read while I was to be away. What a great idea. She presented them to me the morning before I left town. I figured I would read one each day, as time permitted. Each colorful envelope I reached for at any given moment bestowed sheer joy upon me and kept me pleasantly surprised. They were all just what I needed on the days and at the times I opened them.

On the first day, as we were nearing Anchorage, the captain of the aircraft came on the overhead speaker and informed us that the natural light display of the Aurora Borealis was visible from our window seats. What on earth? Well, technically I was no longer on earth, so let's rephrase that: What in heaven's

name? A glorious display of God just doing what He does —
amazing mankind with Him awesomeness. Beautiful, myste-
rious shadows of colors, blending to an Artist's rendition of
glory. Captivating indeed.

When we finally landed in Anchorage, I remembered the
gift of notes that I had safely tucked into my carry-on bag and
decided to open my first one while waiting for my luggage. As
God always orchestrates things with magnificent perfection,
my first message was a verse selected from the Book of James:
"Every good and perfect gift is from above, coming down from
the Father of the heavenly lights, who does not change like
shifting shadows" (1:17). Oh my! He kicked off that trip in
stunning style. After you have seen the heavens dance, you
can praise Him so easily.

A few days into the trip, some of the ladies went horseback
riding. I decided to stay back at the hotel to read and study. I
was also praying for one thing: to see a moose. Never having
seen one in the wild, and knowing that the wildlife in Alaska
was supposed to be so amazing, I just thought I'd ask for one.
I wanted to experience *National Geographic* up close and personal. Oh please, Lord.

A very short time later, I glanced out of the window and
saw a moose and a bonus: her baby calf. The mother and her
young one were at the base of a large hill, starting to ascend.
I didn't have my camera with me, so you'll have to trust me
with this. I dropped my books and headed out back. I started
climbing the hill with them, not permitting them to leave my
sight. The mother kept her pace. The calf stopped a time or
two and looked back to see if I was still coming. She wanted

to play. So did I. But that mother may not be so keen on a play date. I was one third of the way up the large hill when common sense kicked in. *Descend, Nancy. This is their world, not yours. Remember one very important thing – you are not a moose.* Awwww, don't you dislike reality sometimes?

I watched as they headed into the thick forest without me. Oh, the goodness of His Majesty to permit me the privilege to take a moose walk.

The beauties of creation continued to show off the entire time we were in Alaska. All five senses were on overload. A seal in the harbor. The first Alaskan snowflake to fall that season hit the end of my tongue first; I am sure of it. The greatest, freshest, tastiest halibut I have ever had the privilege of being served. The sound of so many women singing praises to the Lamb who is Worthy of all praise. Singing "The King is Coming" as if it were ushering Him back to earth. Oh Glory!

THE BIG "H"

At the youthful age of forty-nine, my mother had a hysterectomy. Back in those days we didn't talk quite as openly as we do now about things, so I don't really remember the circumstances leading up to Mother's surgery. She seemed to sail through the adverse time with no complaining, as was her usual custom.

Six weeks after her surgery we moved overseas. As we were busy setting up for our new assignment, Mom tried to squeeze between a railing and the ladder leading to the attic upstairs and apparently opened the almost-healed incision. She cried out a little and simply said, "It's the Big H." And that's when the name for hysterectomy in our family changed to "Big H."

Then I became fifty and faced the same surgical procedure as my mother had so many years ago. Old memories came to mind, as I mentally prepared to lose a few organs I was given in utero. There was a form of grieving going on inside of me.

The night before my surgery I was washing dishes quite late in the evening, remembering the organ that housed five lives and sustained two for forty weeks. Saying goodbye was quite a process for me. I wondered if my mother had similar thoughts.

In the late and extremely quiet part of the evening, I thought it time to get to bed. Tomorrow's hospital run was an early one. At once I sensed two arms escorting me from the kitchen to the bedroom. They held me under my arms in a very secure way. Confidently I was led forth to rest. They brought me all the way to my bedroom. I felt these strong angels release me into my bed. I couldn't see them, but I knew they were there. As I crawled under the covers, I gave thanks one last time for the fifty years of goodness those inner organs served so faithfully and was now ready to let them go. I simply said to God in my last sentence of the night, "Those angels were a nice touch. Thanks." I truly believe He provided what I needed at that very minute to get me to the next step of the process. How thoughtful "I am with you always..."

COLOMBIA

My second mission trip took me to Colombia, South America. About fifteen of us traveled to this Spanish-speaking country to construct a house for a family of seven very grateful people, provide much needed dental care for the suffering, offer relief preaching by our Spanish-speaking leader, and lead two ladies' events. They were an incredible group of brothers and sisters to be connected with.

The capital of Colombia is Bogotá, a very large city of roughly eight million people. We were assigned to the hills, overlooking the sprawling capital. It has been my experience that, generally, wealthier people take up residence in higher elevations because of the view. Not so here. This area was reserved for the outcasts, the marginalized, and those living in abject poverty.

After a harrowing forty-five-minute drive (fast, crazy, unsafe drivers) to our worksite for the next ten days, we saw those who had such great need. The sights were appalling, unforgettable, and motivating.

Before we began our various duties, we stopped in one of the churches that had been recently built. The structure was a two-story building with the sanctuary on the main floor and classrooms on the upper floor. Wanting to be alone, I ascended the twenty stairs to try to envision rooms full of people gaining life-changing truths, singing to the Most High, and lives being enriched by community.

I found myself by an open window, gazing out at a man seated on his roof, across the dirt street. He was dressed in an old tweed jacket and was just staring. Such a blank stare with the look of hopelessness on his face. I wondered if he worshipped here. I wondered if he knew of Jesus' sacrifice. I began to weep openly. Tears came easily in this place. So much pain comes with the impoverished. I was immediately reminded of the words from Luke 19:41, as I took in the view of the mountains in the distance, the little concrete houses, and this hopeless man. "As Jesus approached and saw the city, He wept over it." I more fully understood the heart of Jesus, as I stood there before that open window.

Just then I was startled by other team members who had climbed the stairs to tour the church. A diminutive brown-skinned man stood tall with my team. He was introduced as the pastor, with the Spanish sounding name "Hey-sus." He tried to correct the Spanish pronunciation of his name to the name of my Savior... with the English pronunciation, saying, "But you can just call me Jesus." *Ah, no. Hey-sus works just fine for me, thank you.* Funny exchange. He was just trying to be helpful.

I worked on the dental team, alleviating incredible pain brought on when people don't have access to all we have here in this country. The hours were long, the lines of people needing assistance were unending, but relief came to the people one by one.

Only one thing could have kept me from going on this trip. My 27th wedding anniversary to Ron fell during this time. We had never been apart for our anniversary before. I was reading the very encouraging cards and notes my daughter again supplied to me; this time she had recruited my friends to each write one. How I loved those cards. So many dear, kind, thoughtful people wrote their sweet and relevant messages to make my days a brighter place. I looked for Ron's hand-written envelope that day, so at least I had a gift from him on September 16th.

Surprise of surprises: when I arrived at our makeshift clinic that morning, the dentist gave me an anniversary gift. Instead of "assisting" him, he let me pull a tooth. Haaaaaaaaa! He gave me what he had to give: an instrument and instructions. I got a firm grasp on the tooth that needed to be pulled and *voila* — it flew across the room. Slippery, slimy thing. Never thought about holding on to it. Maybe I should have; what anniversary does Hallmark say porcelain is for?

Another task I was afforded was to prepare an encouraging talk for the ladies of two villages. It was titled simply "Loving God." At the first church we had so many women arrive that our ladies had to stand outside. The men from our team served the ladies a drink and dessert, which went over *really* well, as they had never seen this in their culture. Women were always serving the men. I was so proud of our guys. Sweets served with smiles.

There was not a single wasted inch in that place. I waited outside in the freezing cold evening as they were finding more and more places to put the women. The hospitality team had cut out snowflake-looking paper decorations to adorn the church building. So festive. They welcomed us so warmly with authentic arms outstretched. What a privilege to be invited into their midst.

I presented the words God had given to me for these dear hearts. The missionary on the ground there, Mark, was my translator. When I inserted a laugh or two he chuckled like I did—how precious. And here I thought laughter was an international language. Those women did not take their eyes off me the entire time. We are all so hungry for God's love, if we would only acknowledge it. These women came as they were—transparent, no pretense, no acting—just themselves. How refreshing.!

After the first event, one lady came up to me with her young son, babbling emotionally to me in Spanish. She was crying as she held this seven-year-old boy. Her plea was full of passion, but I had no idea what she was trying to convey to me. I asked for Mark to come over and translate for me. He said her son was dying. She needed a prayer, an immediate prayer for his healing. As only a mother can demand. We held each other and bawled as we lifted this little guy before the Healer, me in English and her in Spanish. I have no idea what happened after that, but I was shaken by His powerful presence that evening. *Something* took place then. "He heals the brokenhearted and binds up their wounds" (Psalm 147:3). I am sure of it. I pray God healed the boy at that very hour! The emotion of that moment has never left me.

The next woman's conference was much the same, only even more ladies crammed in that place than in the other church. The pastor felt prompted to give an invitation to receive Jesus afterward, and behold, several professed belief in Christ. He is mighty and to be praised for the work He is doing around us and through us. What great encouragement to be part of His Kingdom here on earth.

I am so indebted to those who serve like this daily. Great will be their reward one day. Look for those suffering and make a difference. They are all around us every day. Be their encourager.

The evening before we left for home, a few of us were standing outside the church/dental clinic. It was as if this little building was located at the very end of the world. We had been so busy with the people part of ministry all week that I had only now noticed it was the last building on the street. There was nothing beyond it but green grass as far as the eye could see to the next drop off, which was not visible to us. Somehow pretty. Somehow serene. Somehow strategic?

I asked the pastor who served this small village what was beyond what the eye could see. I was dumbfounded by his reply. "FARC is beyond the hill." *The Revolutionary Armed Forces of Colombia – the People's Army? The guerilla organization? A training camp? Yikes! Was never expecting that reply.* He went on to explain that when they come to overtake Bogotá, which he believes they will, they will come over that grassy area and head straight past this church. The pastor added, "And we will be ready for them!" What a position of faith and vigilance. The Gospel will first be offered. How I pray they have ears to hear the forgiving message.

I had no fear before hearing that, nor any afterward. Jesus commands my destiny, but we are engaged in the fight of a lifetime. Good triumphs over evil because El-Shaddai is greater.

ONE SNOWY NIGHT IN MASSACHUSETTS

A very dear friend had gone in for a routine colonoscopy when she was in her fifties. A polyp was discovered and removed. She was sent home, and all was good, or so we thought. She had some soup and a sandwich for lunch. Within hours she was bent over in excruciating pain. Her husband immediately brought her back to the hospital.

Testing proved that a tiny puncture in her colon from the removal of the polyp was permitting waste to enter her system at will. She endured CT scans almost daily, and infection specialists were called in to help. Apparently, when a sepsis condition compromises the body it is incredibly difficult to treat. Poisons can go multiple places very rapidly. It was a painful, tricky, ever-changing predicament for my dear friend to be in. She was losing health by the hour. She was hospitalized for a total of twenty-five days.

I was about a thousand miles away in Kentucky, and she was in Massachusetts. What was I to do? Ann appeared to be dying. I scrambled to head north that January, but a huge snowstorm blocked my plans. Ugh! A mutual friend made a brief visit to her and reported it was a very grave situation.

I placed a call to the hospital room and heard the very faint, far away, almost inaudible voice of Ann. She recognized me, and after a few pleasantries were exchanged, I asked her about spiritual matters. I have always loved her since the day I first met her, but we had never fully shared the same faith. She initiated the conversation with, "I have been looking for Jesus, but I don't know where to find Him." Gulp. Now is the time of salvation! Behold, today is the day! I had never heard such an openness and willingness from her. We all knew the battle had been long and hard. We needed a happy ending.

I promptly called her daughter. Today was the *only* day she was not planning on venturing all the way out to that rural hospital. When I told her of the conversation I had just had with her mother, she immediately changed her plans and rushed to the hospital. Jeanne is a strong believer and knew the opening for this discussion was upon her.

When Jeanne arrived, her mother and father greeted her in their normal fashion. Ann mentioned that she didn't think her daughter was coming for a visit that night. Jeanne proceeded to lead her willing mother to Christ that night by taking the posture of a sinner in need of a Savior.

I was teaching my Bible study that evening at church, and I shared with them the scene I knew was unfolding in the north. We prayed and finished our lesson. All of the ladies said they were not going to bed until they heard from me. I had given Jeanne strict instructions to call me after all had been won.

Yes, this story has a happy ending. Ann accepted Jesus, her final destination will be Heaven one day, and she was released from the hospital by the end of the week, never to return. Dying to self is always a painful path to travel, but it gives way to living abundantly. On January 25, 2005, after twenty-five years of praying for the salvation of my friend, God made His move. His timing is always perfect and His ways are always so much higher. Some of the craziest circumstances yield the greatest of stories.

Mammy's House

Mammy, Papa, and kids

Mammy and family in backyard

Mom and Dad's
honeymoon, 1947

Mammy's decorative
Swedish coffee pot

Dad, 1971

Mammy's backyard

Becky, Mina, Nancy, Artie, Ron – Mammy's backyard

The Plate

The Renewal

Family time

Mom, 2013

American-Vietnamese students

Becky and Nancy

Ron and Nancy, Big Island

Ron and Bobby, Black Sand Beach

Bobby's family

International students Adjoa and Eric

Mom's 90th birthday with her kids

Joanne, Gordon, Nancy, and Carole

Family in Joanne's backyard

Jim/Joanne's kids – Jonathan and Melanie

Gordon/Adele's daughter, Joanna

Becky, Ron, Nancy and Scott

Ron and Scott

Becky and Mike's wedding, 2011

Nancy and Scott

Ron and Ms. Nerma

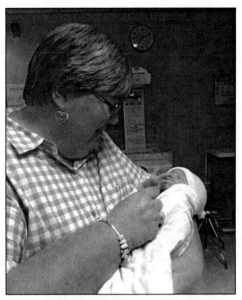

Nanny and Silas, Day #1

Scott and Becky

The Butter Babes

MS. HELEN

One of my seasons in life was spent caring for the dearest group of people: the elderly. They generally appreciate every little thing you do for them. Aging has to be one of the toughest natural processes to embrace, and it comes when we are the weakest and most vulnerable. Some do it gracefully, and others not so much.

I received a call from the office, asking if I would be able to care for a ninety-three-year-old named Helen. Her care would involve taking her to have her hair done and grocery shopping. It was a three-hour assignment. Because her regular caregiver was on vacation, I accepted the assignment. Helen was a Jewish widow. Her condo proudly proclaimed her Jewish heritage. The shelves displaying the scales of justice and law books readily told me her deceased husband had been a lawyer. Helen's demeanor was very brusque and matter of fact.

Much of the reason I started that season in life was due to a Karen Kingsbury book I had read, which gave me a clear directive to make sure all of the older people I would be sent to were on their way to Heaven and nowhere else. I took my assignments very seriously, as I knew those given into my care were in "Heaven's Waiting Room." Some were infirm, depressed, and immobile. But many were jovial, kind-hearted, helpful, and intelligent. I just never knew until I arrived. And I was there to help make their day better for them.

I greeted Helen kindly and tried to create a trusting atmosphere. I asked her if she knew Messiah, trying the direct approach that she seemed accustomed to. She explained that she was Jewish. I had no idea what she meant by that, as Jesus was Jewish too. Maybe it was a connection. She instructed that "there were Jews and there were Jews." Believing she was referring to Orthodox, Reform, Conservative, and Messianic Jews, I was now following her thinking. I told her that I knew that. She seemed surprised. I told her I was a Christian. Primary faith facts were established and then dropped.

We both got into her car without incident, and I was given accurate directions to the hair salon, as this was a weekly outing for her. We went to get her hair washed and set at the salon and then on to the final task of buying groceries that she needed for the following week, me walking and her in her motorized chair. Helen was crippled by rheumatoid arthritis. Her body was very fragile and misshapen, but her mind was extremely sharp. I was helpful in reaching the higher things for her at the store, and she selected things from the lower shelves. We made a good team. After payment was made and food items stored in the trunk, we found satisfaction that we accomplished all she needed to be done that day in a timely fashion and returned home.

She was carefully following the clock, wanting me working all 180 minutes of my shift. With the few remaining minutes, I started cleaning up her kitchen. She informed me it was time to leave, and that she was not paying one nickel beyond what was agreed. I assured her she was not paying any additional fees as I continued to unload her dishwasher. These tasks were easy for me and impossible for her. Why wouldn't I? Working beyond a time clock was a totally foreign concept to dear Helen. After I completed an additional eighteen minutes of "free" work, she told me to look in the refrigerator for a piece of chicken that she wished to give to me. It would be a white breast, as "she didn't like white meat." I think it was a sort of a tip for the extra work I had done for her. I wished her well and left. Yes, I took the chicken, as it would offend her not to. It looked a little older than I would have eaten, so our dog enjoyed every bite. She loved all meat, light and dark.

Two weeks later the office called me and said Helen had called and asked if "Nancy, the Christian" would be available to help her out again. Was I that Nancy? You bet! I went back again and again. I consider that the greatest title I have ever had. Thanks, Ms. Helen.

MAIDEN FLIGHT OF
MY BOEING 777

P aul instructs us in 2 Corinthians 4:7–9, "Now we have this treasure in clay jars, so that this extraordinary power may be from God and not from us. We are pressured in every way but not crushed; we are perplexed but not in despair; we are persecuted but not abandoned; we are struck down but not destroyed." Well, I lived this out in a literal fashion once.

I was flying home from Boston to Louisville one afternoon. This was a maiden voyage for the new Jumbo 777. As I boarded the aircraft, I walked the aisle to find my selected window seat. Since I was the first one in our row, I stowed my belongings in the overhead compartment and took my seat. *Oh my! Tight fit! There is no way I fit on this aircraft. Yikes, what's a gal to do?* I am almost out on the wing at this point, trying to make six inches for my middle seat companion. *This is a toy airplane, not a jumbo. Are you serious?* I was as smashed into a seat as anyone ever could be. My bruised knees were enmeshed into the seat in front of me. It was then that I looked up and saw the 6'9" man who was supposed to fit in the middle seat of this row. I tried not to watch as he painfully contorted into his seat. I tried to make small talk because I think small spaces dictate small talk. He only uttered one word answers back to me. Besides, breathing was becoming an issue. It was at this point I tried to buckle up and realized my seatbelt was a mere 14" too short. I wish I were kidding.

It is the law of flight that passengers use seatbelts. What am I to do? I confessed to my closest friend (literally) that my belt wouldn't fasten. He looked me over and saw how hemmed in I was and remarked, "Honey, you're not going *anywhere!*" And off we went. He was absolutely right. Nothing moved for the duration of the flight. So yes, we were pressured in every way but we were not crushed.

I cannot ever teach on this passage again without thinking of that painful flight and this breakable clay jar.

DREAMS

Do you dream at night? Like bizarre dreams? Things that you can perfectly retell ten years later? How can something that lasts a few seconds take twenty minutes to explain? The details in some of our night visions are preposterous, outlandish. They have the capacity to scare us half to death, comfort us, challenge us, convict us, or even cause us to cry, laugh, or scream. They are the craziest things. Sleep can be an alarming place some nights. And the memories, good or bad, can last a lifetime. I usually dream in living Technicolor and am amply amused at the absurd upon awakening. But everyone in our family has had some doozies at one time or another.

Sleep came easily for our son, Scott. He was a sleepwalker, so he *lived* his dreams. Our active boy studied his lessons by day and ran hard the rest of the afternoon. After dinner was the time set for a slower pace, preparing for bedtime. We always entered the last part of his day with the usual routine: pajamas, brushing teeth, story time, and prayers. It was such a sweet time of our day. Before bed he would relay things that were on his mind or some of the favorite parts of his day. Some nights, as I would kneel beside his bed, my knees began to ache, as his tales were apt to be captivating and quite long. But every night ended with prayers and a kiss goodnight.

Having no idea where Scott would "go" when he drifted off to sleep made for some pretty wild and hilarious adventures that defy explanations.

Many nights one parent or the other would be aroused by a motionless silhouette standing by the head of our bed. *Gee willikers!* To be disrupted out of a deep sleep to find a snoozing frozen figure twelve inches from our faces was quite alarming indeed. We would gently guide him back to his bed, cover him, and return to our bed. When interrogated the following morning, "Hey Scott, do you remember your midnight stroll last night?" His answer was also the same. "Nope." What a riot.

One night Ron went in to check on him before heading to bed and found him sound asleep under some towels, comforter missing. When Scott reached the breakfast table the next morning Ron inquired, "Son, why were you covered in towels last night?" Scott matter-of-factly responded, "I was cold. I have no idea where my comforter is." Where on earth could a queen-sized spread be?

After some time, the comforter was located: jammed and stuffed under the coffee table in the living room. The diligent work of a persevering rodent or eager beaver could not have done a more precise job in hiding the comforter. Skillful undertaking. We surmised that when he got back in his bed and got cold, he went into the linen closet and grabbed a few towels to keep warm, and that was it. For a period of time we had been observing sporadic sleepwalking patterns with our son, so we were amused and sorry we missed "the show."

Another morning we were awakened by a terrified young boy screaming, "I'm blind! I can't see a thing!" Rushing to his bedroom, and fighting the laughter welling up inside of us, Becky and I discovered that Scott had his head inside of his pillowcase. As we arrived, he placed his hands on his "face" and shrieked, "My face is fabric!" Oh my. Removing the bed linen from his head transformed his green plaid expressionless face into fleshy cheeks and restored sight. His rapidly beating heart slowed, and his smile returned to his handsome face.

Becky had a nightmare once that I was zippered up — that one still freaks her out to this day. Ron remembers me screaming in the middle of the night a few times (with windows open). I had no recollection of what was going on. Ron has killed people and has gone to such happy places — not in the same dream, of course. I have dreamt of polar bears pursuing me, saving the day, losing someone close, and even have had great dreams that I wish were real: people who have died have visited me and comforted me. It was so great being with them and seeing them again.

Our minds are powerful devices. Vivid images convincingly appear, but they are not even real. And of course some people don't remember their dreams at all. I wonder which is better — to dream or not to dream (and remember)? Not that we have a say in things.

We know that some dreams have profound power and life-changing capabilities, but our family has never had any of those. Ours are purely of the entertaining variety.

ETHIOPIA

My third mission trip was to Jimma, Ethiopia. The nature of this mission was medical, educational, and evangelical. Life in Abundance is a solid, Christ-centered body of talented people who give to those with less and anticipate God's greatness at every turn. I am most impressed with how they all conducted their daily, disciplined lives. Such a wonderful example of always putting God first and praying about everything.

Upon our arrival, many people lined up on one side of the building that would become our clinic for the next ten days to welcome us. They were darling, excited, and most generous in their gestures. As I approached the doorway of this structure, an animated lady in an elaborate white dress and head scarf reached for me, jabbering on in Amharic while hugging my neck. Her eyes were wild with excitement. While I really had no idea what she was saying because of the language barrier, I felt a very strong connection to her. I asked one of the local doctors if she was a Christian, and he said she was. I choose to believe it was the Holy Spirit saying, "Hey Nancy! Welcome!"

A holy hug from the Holy One. Welcome to Africa. What a reassuring and unique greeting that was.

Our welcome ceremony consisted of local coffee, as Jimma is the coffee capital of Ethiopia, and popcorn. A dear servant carefully roasted the beans over an open flame on the floor. The townspeople entered the building but were not invited to sample the food or drink. We sat across from these locals while they just stared, nodded, and smiled at us. The very community that had so little to offer gave everything they had. Doc Paul and I were the only two non-coffee drinkers, but you better believe we drank that entire demitasse of strong brew to show our appreciation. And we loved every drop.

The first day we opened our "clinic" we had people lined up as far as the eye could see. I was filling medications for those who had need, when suddenly I was called away by the local team's evangelist to pray with a beautiful young lady. We were working in a predominately Muslim population, during the month of Ramadan. (Ramadan is one of the five pillars of Islam and involves fasting for thirty days during daylight hours.) I asked the team's evangelist how I could pray for her. He said, "She wants to become a Christian." Tears rolled down my cheeks, as I was privileged to lead this darling sister into the faith. We had more than fifty professions during our time there. The fields were so ready for harvest.

We visited eight churches in nine days, and I was honored to present the truth of God's Word to the ladies of the land. My dear translator, "T," never seemed to tire in his vital role of taking the message, translating it, and blessing those ladies. By the fourth church, he said in flawless English that his wife needed this message of hope and that he was going to tell her everything I had said. I honestly think he memorized the entire talk. So hungry for hope are we all.

Upon entering each church, one lady would stand up and speak in her native tongue a blessing over us and the words that would be spoken to them. What a great encouragement that was for me personally. The other attendees all spoke in agreement with whatever she was asking or declaring. Such a powerful witness before the Lord! I have never forgotten that beautiful custom, which blessed me so greatly.

Our days were full and inspiring, as we all felt the Lord's presence and power in our work and our newly formed relationships. One afternoon a team member, who was testing eyesight and distributing glasses, asked if I would go back and pray for a man. She just didn't feel comfortable in that role, so I went into the back room, and she replaced me in the front room.

I was cordially welcomed into the room by the translator, a man named Immanuel. His name literally means "God with us." Yes, sir. My heart was rejoicing and tickled at the thought of his mother choosing the very best for her son. His face beamed with the radiance of Christ.

Immanuel began to inform me that a middle-aged couple, seated on the bench with their backs to me, requested prayer. The man had asked for prayer for his heart, which had "fire" in it and for his aching knees. On my shallow, human level, I thought heartburn and possibly arthritis. Without making eye contact with the man, I placed my hands on the back of his shoulders and began the prayer of sincere faith—not really understanding the whole fire in the heart thing, but being obedient nonetheless. As I offered the first line of praise, I hesitated and waited for Immanuel to translate the first line to our patient. Nothing. *Okay, then I will pray about what I don't understand over a man I will never know in a language he does not comprehend.* How atypical are the dealings of God sometimes.

As I started to passionately petition Almighty God on behalf of this man, my hands began to move — at first gently, then more violently. This fellow was convulsing. I opened my eyes to make sure everything was fine with him. What on earth was going on? Immanuel had his head still bowed, eyes closed, in the posture of prayer he had begun with. I decided to keep going. I was still working on the fire in his heart and hadn't even gotten to his knees yet. I was wondering if there were demons involved, so I called for power to win over any darkness around us. No wonder my teammate left this to me! Such an unusual assignment. After about fifteen minutes of praying over everything I knew to pray for, with the guidance of the Holy Spirit, I closed things down in the name of Jesus. Things were calm again. I thanked Immanuel for being there (and for God making sure someone named Immanuel was assigned to that role), and I went back to the front room, never having seen the faces of that couple.

The night before our departure, seventeen of us sat around a table and discussed the highs and lows of our time together. A few of the local missionaries were excitedly discussing a story that involved the "man with fire in his heart." I overheard and just had to ask them what that phrase meant, as I had encountered that exact phrase earlier in the week. They said that "the preacher" was back! Apparently this man was "on fire" for God but grew very discouraged about ten years ago when so many overwhelming problems faced him, and God seemed distant and uncaring. So he walked away from the faith.

When we came to his town to help, he saw God at work. He returned to his faith and was now back and willing to disciple the more than fifty converts God had just dished up for him to lead. Yes, he was the man I had been asked to pray over. The convulsing, I am now sure of, was a decade of pent up sorrow and repentance before God. *Would You please take me back on Your team? I am so sorry for doubting You! I will never leave the faith again. I have seen the Lord.* We confess. He forgives and cleanses. What a deal. It now made perfect sense. The man's repentance traveled through my hands into my love-saturated heart. What a mighty God we serve.

On our last day after everything was packed up, I looked around that small building and thought of all the health, hope, and help that had been accomplished in the last ten days and prayed the missionaries and townspeople forward in their mission to show people the way to Jesus.

Just then a native was standing in the doorway, listening to my last audible prayer. A huge smile stretched across his worn, brown face. He motioned to grab my bag, desiring to carry it to the bus at the curb for me. In an instant, the Holy Spirit introduced us: it was the preacher! He had recognized my voice and knew I was the one who prayed him back to the Lord's good grace. Be still my soul! We walked, hugged, and knew a special God allowed us to meet face to face, this side of Eternity. Grateful is an understatement! Carry on, Preacher Man. You have been forgiven and found worthy by Jesus.

MS. POLLY

Ms. Polly was another dear elderly friend I enjoyed some time with. She had fallen prey to Alzheimer's disease. Although she lived in a fine facility to assist the elderly, her son wanted someone with her so she would not be alone or isolated. I was assigned twelve-hour shifts with Ms. Polly. She was as grace-filled as you would wish for a ninety-something woman. I introduced myself and asked what she enjoyed doing. As she fumbled for a tangible response, I realized I would need to fully plan our first day together. We left her apartment and walked a short distance and sat to watch the ducks swim in the pond. It was a serene, peaceful place of tranquility. We watched as the "bread man" came to feed the hungry, grateful ducks. I introduced the familiar passage from Matthew 6 in which Jesus tells us to look at the birds of the sky. They don't sow or reap or gather into barns, yet our heavenly Father feeds them and that we are worth more than they are. It struck a very familiar chord in her. It brought a form of peace over both of us. Her reaction revealed God's touch on her life.

After a while we headed back to her place for her mid-day meal in the dining area. I too would be served, being Ms. Polly's guest. *I think I will grow to love this assignment.* We prayed, ate, enjoyed fellowship with other residents, and said our good-byes. We walked outside to another area. Finding a quaint and fanciful bench beneath a beautiful oak tree, we delighted in the moment afforded us. The clouds were especially beautiful that day, so I insisted that we play a game of naming objects that the clouds resembled. You have never had as much fun with this game as when you have played it with an aged child. She was uninhibited, creative, and saw what she joyously saw. We saw a bookshelf, a baby, a planet, a squirrel, a mountain range, a monkey (doesn't everyone see a monkey?), trains... the real and the imagined. What a wonderful time we had under the expansive blue and white sky. Chuckles came with every new shape, as we would try to see what the other was seeing. I am not sure we matched on too many shapes. But how gratifying it was just being together.

As the clock was close to striking three, we entered the facility to attend "Poetry and Tea at Three" — the activity that was scheduled for that day. We were invited to bring a poetry book and read, if we desired. Ms. Polly did not want to take a book to the event, although she had hundreds in her room. So we went empty-handed but full-hearted.

As we were sipping our hot herbal tea, one ninety-five-year-old tablemate read a beautiful poem from her book. Then a ninety-eight-year-old recited *ten verses* from memory. A frail, kind woman to my right asked if I could read her selection for her, as her eyesight was "not what it used to be." I eagerly accepted. Her age? One hundred and three. Goodness gracious! I want to be like these charming ladies when/if I ever become a nonagenarian. Ladies of wit, wisdom, and grace. How I enjoyed my tea that day with those darling gals.

Ms. Polly and I ended our first afternoon outside. It really was such a beautiful day—the kind of day you want to be outside every moment you are permitted. I found a subject that she simply loved talking about: her husband, so we stayed on that topic for some time. I heard about the greatest man to ever enter her life. She loved him with every part of herself and would join him for all eternity. He had gone on ahead of her, so there was sadness in her days (coupled with the terrible disease she must endure a while longer). But she was still yearning for Heaven. I found myself interviewing her and carefully monitoring her answers. Whether they were strictly accurate or not, it somehow didn't matter. She loved this guy, and I needed to pay attention to every word that came from her heart through her mouth. I asked her what the hardest part of being married was. She simply answered, "Nothing." She loved every minute of it. Of course I know better, but what may be my response in a few years? I pray it is covered in the grace hers was.

After dinner I safely left her in her cozy home, dressed for bed. I prayed over her and told her I would see her in the morning. She smiled and patted me on the arm. After twelve hours with this little lamb, introducing and reintroducing myself to her, I asked her one question before leaving. "Do you remember my name?" Sadly, she did not. That too did not matter.

We would play new games tomorrow, and we would find God in that day too. He promised to be with her until she is again joined with Mr. Wonderful and stands healthy and healed in God's presence. She taught me a very valuable lesson that day: every day lived to the glory of God is a day well lived indeed.

And yes, she's home now with those she loves. Thanks, Ms. Polly.

POLAND

My fourth mission trip was to the wonderful country
of Poland. A small but hilarious team of six crazy
ladies—Patsy, Sandie, Linda, Annette, Jo, and I—headed
east at the appointed time. We were to join our Polish church
partners in presenting a women's conference to ladies from
Poland and Ukraine. Every team, I have noticed, is just perfectly put together. This group was no different. So off to
Zakosciele we went.

PROeM, our ministry partner there, attracts some of the
nicest people you will ever meet. And such gracious hosts. We
were cared for, loved, fed well, and welcomed as royalty. They
are some of the hardest working people around. And without
complaint. They were great witnesses and loved sharing their
giftedness with the world.

Because of space issues, we were to give the same three-day
conference twice with a day off in between. It was my sheer
delight being in ministry with those dearly beloved sisters.

In one of my breakout sessions, I had both Polish and
Ukrainian ladies, so I needed two interpreters for both languages. That was a stretch: after I said something, it was

translated to Polish, then into Ukrainian, and then I forgot where I was. Haaaaaaa! Oh, the long-reaching effects of the Tower of Babel...

I was coaching these darling ladies on the need to be actively engaged in a Bible study and how essential it was to our growth and central to living Godly lives. I was sharing with them about the next Bible study I was asking the Lord about leading, thousands of miles away from these dear women. The Ukrainian translator stopped, turned to me, and asked which one it was. I informed her. Shockingly, she stated, "I knew it!" and promptly informed us that she had just returned from England where she had recently completed translating into Ukrainian the same study. There really are no such things as coincidences.

Relationship is a gift; I am convinced of it. So is laughter. Much of life is predictable and routine. Our team leaned in to our own *Truman Story*. We acted out our own screenplay.

Every morning at 7:55 AM Sandie would knock on my door and ask to borrow my antiperspirant. I would take two steps to the right, grab it, and hand it to her. She would apply and hand it back. Every. Single. Day. It. Played. Out. Exactly. The. Same. Way. By day three, I was standing just inside the door waiting for her knock. Like clockwork. She tapped her knuckles. The commonplace became hysterical. We both couldn't control our giggles.

Breakfast was always downstairs at 8:30 AM. Cold cuts, cheeses, tomatoes, hot tea, and bread. Such wonderful fare. To change things up, we sat at various tables.

Between the conferences our Polish friends took us to Krakow (pronounced Krack-off). It was such a beautiful old European city. Our hotel was very modern and comfortable. The only problem was morning; not being a morning person, it is hard to coexist with those who like to sing in the morning. Annette came early to check on me. In keeping with our rhyming games that week, my opening line of the day was "Yes, we're in Krack-off, so back-off!" Again, hysteria!

On our off day in Krakow, we were in a mostly vacant, beautifully-lit city square. Colorful flags attached to slender, silver flagpoles adorned this exquisite open space. Lighting from deep within the walkway gave just enough light to enhance and give brilliance to these majestic flags. Patsy and I saw fit to do a little "pole dancing" — seeing as how we were walking among the towering flagpoles in Poland and all. Our unbendable, immovable, metal, dance partners stood their ground while we danced around them in the lovely city square. So if anyone ever asks if I have pole danced, I reply that I have. It is a real résumé booster!

Walking through St. Mary's Basilica was breathtaking. This magnificent fourteenth-century structure, still functioning, had an elaborate interior that is a true work of art. The colors, the sculptures that tell a story, and the overwhelming attention to details take up residence in one's heart. It did have, however, a very unusual ritual every hour. A lone trumpeter would make his appearance in the high tower and play the same partial song every sixty minutes. Suddenly, he'd end with an abrupt half-note and walk back inside the door. It commemorated an unknown bugler who was struck in the throat with an arrow as he tried to warn his people from advancing invaders many years ago. We stayed two hours so we could see this unique tribute played out twice in exactly the same way.

We had so many unique and fun experiences on our trip. Roasting Polish kielbasa in Poland over an open fire was a first. We treated our guests to a pampering session with haircuts, manicures, and massages. And we strolled the beautiful grounds of our campsite, making connections and memories for a lifetime. God, bless Poland!

BUTTER BABES

Several years ago, God brought me a bouquet of beauties named Bonnie, Elizabeth, and Fay, affectionately called the Butter Babes. They are genuinely great, Godly, giving, and generous girlfriends. It is a gift from the Lord to share life with them. As there are four sticks of butter in a package, so we came together as a package deal. How we actually acquired the name must remain veiled to protect an anonymous innocent. Trust me on that.

We deepened our relationship with outings, eatings, talkings, meetings, and beings. We are so different in personality, backgrounds, and family make ups, which makes for delightful and stimulating conversations. These are the girls that are always there for you. You may call at any time or group text an urgent prayer request or praise, and encouragement is instantaneous. We all have different spiritual gifts, so we lean in frequently to the one who needs to rise at a given time to lead the pack.

A mutual friend of ours heard from all sides how much fun we were having, doing, and sharing. And so there were five! We affectionately call Judy, our eldest member, "Butter Superior." She adds a whole new layer of grace and giftedness to the Babes.

We all have a great desire to laugh and be tickled by sharing the various stories and silly circumstances we find ourselves in. So, we began the tradition of bring "butter" gifts to our meetings. Creative gifting is an understatement. Body butter, butter rum lifesavers, Butterfinger candy bars, cans of butter beans, butter mints, Mrs. Butterworth's syrup, and so much more. At Thanksgiving we were all given turkey-sculpted butter for our tables. Butter-molded Christmas trees followed a month later. We even got a mat that says, "Well butter me up and call me a biscuit"

One Babe had a "butter party" at her house. We all wore yellow shirts and sampled butter from several different countries spread on all sorts of goodies. I am here to say a cow is not a cow everywhere; butter has varying tastes the world over.

Oh, and alliteration? It is almost a second language for us. It always encourages us to be creative and grow our vocabularies. Once we had a Butter Babes Belated Birthday Bash at the Bountiful Bread Bakery, which may have been a record. I wish I could remember the hundreds of cleverly crafted emails that were sent and received by these delightful, divine dames.

The Bible instructs us to bear one another's burdens. These are those ladies. When Mike and Becky were married in 2011, they all pitched in to design, direct, and decorate. They are the kind of friends you could never pay back and the kind who would never want to be. They carry you and your load to the Father, who gives strength and peace just because of who He is. Having this kind of support makes a world of difference daily.

Glory to God for these gorgeous gals!

CUBA

Okay, let's head 228 miles south of Miami to the nation of Cuba. This beautiful tropical island, the largest in the Caribbean, has roughly eleven million inhabitants and is approximately the size of Pennsylvania.

The year is 2008, the month is November, and the number of travelers not quite fifty. The all-male choir from our church, the Master's Men, will bring their powerful voices to their forthcoming concerts with the Cuban National Choir, and the ladies will bring arts, crafts, supplies, notes, Bibles, and teachings to conduct a women's conference and children's outreach event. Ready. Set. Excited!

At the time, most passengers entered Cuba aboard chartered flights, as not every city permits outbound flights to this communist nation. And that's exactly what we did. We boarded our fifty-passenger, prop commuter airplane. Miami to Havana, direct flight. Short and sweet, right? Wrong.

Technically, we were still in hurricane season, but no one was thinking of inclement weather. Our minds were engrossed in executing memorized stanzas, verses, prayer, or simple conversations with friends close by. The interruptions came simultaneously through turbulence and the broadcast, "This is your captain." Oops! Reality check. We are cruising at 24,000 feet and headed for some terrible, tumultuous turbulence.

Never have I been on a more terrifying, horrendous, hair-raising flight in my life. We *were* going down! Not knowing if our pilot was a thrill-seeker, an adventurer, or new to flying increased my concern. Praying openly and obtrusively to Jesus became my default. It's what you do when you are preparing to meet Him. My mind thought, *Was it really supposed to end this way, Lord?* David came to mind, as I recalled him facing a fierce giant. Only he had a slingshot. I forgot mine at home. But we have the same huge God to fight our fears and battles for us. That horrific experience lasted about thirty minutes. In contrast, eternity lasts forever.

As you can tell by reading this narrative, the plane did not crash into the Caribbean Sea. While I am elated to report we all safely made it to our destination, we had much ahead for us to focus on.

The people of Cuba were warm, welcoming, kind-hearted, and humble in their approach to their returning and new American friends. The pastor we served with, and his family were beyond gracious in every way.

Our accommodations were enjoyable, and the weather was commendable. The feasting should have been illegal. Our cooks arrived every day and gave everything they had, and God added to it. They prepared delicious cuisine for all to enjoy, including my special portion with no onions, due to my allergy. Extremely thoughtful.

Every morning at around 10:00 AM we were served Cuban espresso. Not being a coffee drinker, I was surprised by the delectable brew they had concocted for us. By the end of the ten-day trip my lips eagerly greeted the daily demitasse.

The rehearsals and concerts blended the voices of the two choirs in beautiful harmonies and with one accord. Our men serenaded in Spanish, and the Cubans crooned in our language. Both teams practiced the foreign terms until they sounded flawless together. The music in the beautifully designed basilica was almost heavenly.

Family was forming fast. Every day we were handed blessing after blessing from our Father and the fine folk of Cuba.

One day a small team went to evangelize the underserved in the projects close by. The huge, towering, dilapidated living quarters stood as giants before us. Idle people hung out of their windows, watching life from a distance. The few children we observed were filthy, their clothes torn and tattered, and their bellies empty. Oh, but their smiles shone brighter than the noonday sun. Those children had been sentenced to an impoverished state, yet they rose above their circumstances. The magic of a child's spirit is that hope is placed in them and God watches over them.

We encountered the Bread Man on our walk. How fortunate. A loaf of bread for a nickel. How blessed to have had a few nickels and not any hunger. The small loaves were given to a few destitute folk, and others were stuffed into my pockets for later.

Our translator took us to one apartment after another to share God's love with them. What an opportunity to share hope with the hopeless. One flat was home to an older woman and her family. They graciously permitted us entrance and listened eagerly to God's promises and peace amid difficult times. The gift of bread was carefully and discreetly placed on the counter. The older hungry woman spotted it and could not focus on anything except the food that had been given to her family. She received the Bread of Life that day, as well as her daily bread. Feast time. Go, Jesus!

We visited a family in another complex. The translator brought us there because it was his family. We were again accepted graciously. Small talk began. Those of us not proficient in Spanish waited to hear of conversation we could join in on. I caught an older, weathered man (I believe it was our young translator's grandfather) staring at me. Smile. Stare. Smile. *What is this, Lord?* I noticed his rugged hands, somewhat gnarled through time. I walked across the small room, took his hands, and he stood up, opposite me. As I held these hands I prayed over them aloud in English, not having a clue why. He understood nothing of what I was saying.

Suddenly all was quiet in the room. The translator began to give the old man my intercessory words in his heart language. He began to cry. I began to cry. We hugged. We left.

On the way down the stairway, I asked the kid what his grandfather did. He proudly said, "He was a doctor." His hands had healed, delivered babies, and walked through life hand in hand with his beautiful wife until she walked into Heaven's gate. Now that he was older, and due to the restrictions of the Communist government, those hands just changed lightbulbs from time to time. Such a travesty. But once a doctor, always a doctor; I *know* he still practices, even if he no longer has a license or access to medical facilities.

God knew that man needed to know those hands were still valued. And so He sends us out to accomplish whatever it is He needs us to do. Who can know the mysteries of Christ?

Kids came from all over to our Creation Outreach. Kids love everything. Bubbles to blow, pages to color, crayons to color with, crafts to be crafted, snacks to be enjoyed, laps to sit in, hugs to be had…

Our women's conference had the theme Hands, Heart, and Hope. Sounds great, right? I love alliteration, only in Spanish it became *Manos, Corazon, Esperanza*—not the same effect as I was shooting for. Ha! Oh well, I will consider translation next time. But the ladies didn't seem to care. They delighted that we were there, loving them, teaching them, pampering them, playing games with them, feeding them, and enjoying our time together. Laughter translates well in all languages.

At the third and final session, I asked if there was anyone who wished to become a follower of Jesus, as we had just finished talking about the heart. I had instructed them to raise their hands if there was a desire to do so. No *manos* went up. They stood. I went outside to the bench in front of the church with the first lady to stand, along with my translator (the pastor's daughter). I asked her if she would lead this beautiful woman to the foot of the cross and lead her in a prayer of repentance. They conversed a while in Spanish, and she stated, "She wants you to talk to and pray for her." I was a bit confused, since I would just tell my translator the spiritual truths she already knew, and she would tell this woman, so why was I in the equation?

You know that moment you should stop your mind from thinking things through and shut your mouth? I was at that point. I explained the plan of salvation and prayed for her, as I was asked to. My translator later told me that sweet lady was her aunt, the pastor's sister. And the woman's brother, the preacher, told me later that day that she wanted to have her own house church in her home. No seminary degree? Nope — the Spirit's enough to lead anyone anywhere they need to go. Have the faith of a child, and He can take you places you never imagined.

I checked back with the pastor seven years later. A house church had started in her apartment a week after she decided to follow Christ. What a model for obedience and trust. I love the ways of God. They astound, astonish, and amaze.

Finally a little alliteration.

Oh, and when we arrived back at the airport, a beautiful 747 with a seasoned pilot sat at the gate, welcoming its elated passengers. Smooth ride home. *Manos* used. *Corazons* full. *Esperanza* unshakable.

THE BIRDS

Laughter is one of the greatest medicines. It can cure whatever ails you—like mornings. Pre-dawn hours are of no interest to me, unless laughing with my child is involved. When our son, Scott, was in middle school, the morning routine went as follows: his rooster alarm "crowed" at 5:50 AM. He would promptly arise, make his bed, dress for school, and meet his father at the breakfast table for cereal. There was very little verbal exchange, as Scott didn't care for mornings either.

Please take notice of who was *not* in the morning picture: me. I tried getting up, but it just would not happen. So, an unusual pattern developed. After all morning chores were completed and our son was fed, Scott would come to my bed and slip under the covers (fully dressed), on his father's side. You see, I could talk, just not arise. Oh, what joy filled my soul as he joined me every morning. Greeting, meeting, chatting, relaxing, and laughing were in order every school day, until Ron would call for his car rider at 6:45 AM.

With the chilly air wafting through the open window in the still of the morning, we began to focus on the birds that were chirping, calling, and cackling outside. Such cheap entertainment. Focusing on what they may be saying, we attuned our hearing to listen a little more attentively. Most mornings the cry of the "wirty bird" was most prominent. "Wirty, wirty, wirty," he unceasingly sang. Then the "thank you bird" would chime in. He had the most grateful voice ever. This feathered creature with perfect pitch and a unique, squeaky voice and excellent intonations simply stated over and over again, "thank you, thank you, thank you." How could we not be more grateful after hearing the "early birds" serenading us like this?

Listening more carefully, we both thought the garage door raised up, as that familiar creak of the rail that needed lubrication screamed metal on metal—but no, we had discovered another bird outside. The screamer had come for a visit. It is amazing how we matched birds with every kind of sound that interrupted the silence of the morning. Oh, the laughter and most humorous comments imaginable came forth those early mornings.

One morning things were so out of control and we were giggling so loud that Becky came out of her room (her classes started later than her brother's) to find out what was so comical. Becky knew of our morning merriment but never cared to join in, as she dislikes mornings more than I do. But one day she just had to get in on it. As soon as we saw her dark silhouette, we just exploded! I wonder what the birds thought of our howling hymn that morn. Looking on the lighter side of life before the sun rose set the tone for a better day for all.

When Scott was in his twenties, high atop a ladder outside in the early part of the day, he heard the "wirty bird" calling out to him. Of course he had to call his mother and let her know of his good fortune.

Our birds are still singing. We are still listening. They may succeed our original music makers by twenty generations, but their message is still the exact same. Make good memories — they last a lifetime.

APPALACHIA

I was privileged to travel with several mission partners to the poorer section of Kentucky a few years ago. It is hard to conceive the third-world living conditions that exist in this country, approximately four-and-a-half hours' drive from Louisville.

These dear, rural, proud, mountain people do not generally have access to many things we city folk have at our fingertips. Roughly 750 doctors, nurses, pharmacists, and laypeople gave up three days to arrange for a mobile medical clinic in the underserved area of our commonwealth.

As an advocate, I was to support, direct, befriend and pray for the patients assigned to me. Brenda was my first. She was a quiet-spirited, no-nonsense sixty-year-old wife, mother, and grandmother, and was very apprehensive about receiving these medical gifts from unknown personnel.

We quickly became friends. I assured her that God brought this roadshow to town for her, and she was welcome to pick and choose the options that appealed to her. The broad offerings included services such as mammograms, pap smears, and eye exams; there was also a camp for kids, family portraits, and free haircuts, among other things.

"If you could choose one thing for yourself today, Brenda, what would it be?" I asked. With waiting and possibly large crowds, I wanted to prioritize her choices. "An eye exam would be my first choice, as I have never had my eyes checked," was her response. In escorting her to the optometrist, we talked of her life experiences, and she told me about her many family members.

She was promptly seen. Volunteers who really wanted to be there make such a difference, in my book. As they evaluated her sight, she was handed a Bible and asked to read what she could see. She couldn't make out a single word. When she was handed a pair of "cheaters," she gasped as if seeing the alphabet for the very first time. The sound of her reading that Ancient Book almost brought tears to my eyes. A whole new world was opening up to her. She had not read anything in years, including her precious Bible. She was given the "cheaters" and the volunteers promised that her prescription would be mailed to her in about two weeks. Overjoyed does not begin to describe her reaction.

Her second desire was to have a mammogram. She had never had a breast exam. She was sixty years old and getting a baseline. So off to the mobile unit we went. She walked in bravely, confidence building with every step. I must confess it felt great to sit in the waiting room and not have to be seen that day. But, it's because I can be seen yearly. So, I took the afternoon off and let Brenda be checked and x-rayed. She was so blessed to be examined. Every year when I *must* go, I remember how it was a sheer privilege for her.

Kentucky Disaster Relief was brought in and had prepared a feast for all. We went through the food line, and our plates were filled with a delicious hot meal. What a huge blessing this was for both of us. Lunch at no cost? So we gave thanks, and enjoyed lunch together.

"Brenda, if you could have three gifts today, what would number three be?" She responded, "I have only had one pap smear in my life, and the doctor was extremely rough with me." I told her that I was sure the doctors here would take better care of her, and took her to the appropriate place. This was her longest appointment, and I prayed all was going okay for her behind those closed doors.

She came out beaming, "They were so nice. They prayed with me, talked with me, examined me... but I knew I should not have come today," Brenda said. I was perplexed. She divulged that during her urinalysis they found some bleeding. I countered, "Well, I am so glad you came today so your health could be restored." And off to the free pharmacy we went. She was outfitted with the prescription she needed, and took the first dose to get things rolling; another gift had been given: medicine.

Being educated in that short span of time, I recognized how shallow I am. I would have decided to have a haircut over a mammogram and would love to have had a picture of myself to bring home more than a cancer screening. But how wise this woman was. Nothing frivolous. Just needs being met. The things that truly matter. Uncomfortable situations over comfort.

Brenda and I had a wonderful experience together that day. She was going home to tell all her family and friends of the most wonderful, charitable, helpful medical attention she had received. It was like she sprouted some wings. Everyone she knew could benefit from something being offered there. They were free to come the following day.

My takeaway that day was to be thankful for all we do have—all that has been given to us in the course of one day—and to value each person God places in our lives, even if they're there for a few hours.

As we parted company, I prayed for her, and she prayed for me. I envisioned God was smiling over both of us, as He directed our whole encounter. All done for His glory is, in fact, a wonderful way to leave it. Give thanks.

MR. AND MRS. H

Bloom where you are planted. Blessed are the flexible; for they shall not be bent out of shape. Important ideas to remember. When I received my orders to enter the home of an older couple, I was ready and willing to serve them as they needed me. They were a most delightful couple, and I loved them right away. They were graceful, kind, likeable, and dear, making my entry into their world effortless.

One thing I love about many older adults is that they usually know what they want and when they want it. Our days together began at 8:00 AM and lasted until 8:00 PM. We did most things at a slower pace to accommodate my dear aging friends.

Mr. H was eleven years older than his bride and was a darling man. He had severe hearing loss, which made it challenging to converse with him, and he was somewhat isolated because of his inability to join most conversations. Finding an old chessboard in a crowded cabinet was the magic remedy. This elderly gentleman's smile radiated throughout the living room when his long-forgotten board and familiar pieces were laid on the table in front of him. Mr. H was a sharp man and loved being challenged. Because he was such a good player, his family had stopped playing this arduous game with him more than twenty years ago. It was nonsensical to keep playing him and losing every game. He was very competitive and way too formidable an opponent for most. He won most every game he played.

It would bring me great joy to be beaten and ego-bruised if Mr. H were happily winning again. So out came his old home-made companion. He told of his great memories and victories won on this 2′ by 2′ wooden slab and gave me pointers on playing strategies. Apparently, when you have achieved such success at this game, it stays with you. He declared victory over me four out of four games during our first competition—and we both could not have been happier. Hour by hour we spent crouched over that little tray table, awaiting our turn, and I treasured in my heart the glorious sight of watching this gentleman come back to life through the complex game of chess.

Upon returning home week after week, I would give my family the dreadful updates that Mr. H continued to win every single game. Then one day it was Mr. H-3, Nancy-1! When you are matched with an adversary one million times better than you, you must improve. And then I would realize I was playing a ninety-two-year-old with failing eyesight—nothing to gloat over.

Mrs. H was a well-read, classy, southern lady who complemented and completed her man. She was a charming conversationalist and most gracious in her approach to others. Sitting with her was always so fulfilling and educational. But she struggled with short-term memory issues in her advanced years.

Every day at 4:30 PM cocktails were to be served. I needed to be instructed on how to make their drinks. Mr. H had a Bloody Mary, and Mrs. H requested a gin and tonic. Check.

When supplies diminished, a trip to the local convenience store was in order. I decided to buy the largest bottles because of the lower price and bought as many as I could handle so I had to make these runs less frequently. As an abstainer from alcohol, it was a little awkward to grab multiple large containers, fill the cart, and proceed toward the checkout area. This was a daunting task, as I gave the appearance of being an alcoholic. Yes, there were some looks. But this was part of my job — to see that my friends were looked after.

After finishing my transaction, I loaded all of the libations into their snazzy Mercedes Benz and headed back to their home. What amused me most was considering the possibility of being identified by one of my Bible study gals or my preacher. What on earth would someone think if they caught me with loads of liquor, racing off in a Mercedes? *So* not the real me. I chuckled as I considered being a little more observant with my surroundings. Wouldn't that be so typical to be seen and not addressed? People and their faulty assumptions...

One night on the news it was reported that the same little convenience store I frequented had its ornamental overhanging roof break and fall to the sidewalk. People entering and exiting at will and then *boom*, gravity had claimed that entryway roof and sign without warning. All I could imagine was what the morning headlines would have been if I were crushed under that sign with hundreds of dollars of liquor in front of that upscale vehicle.

Mr. H asked me one day if I would like to visit his cemetery plot. At such an advanced age, I knew of his need to discuss the sensitive subject of death, so I agreed. I drove the fancy car to a beautiful piece of real estate where he and his wife would be laid to rest one day. We stopped the car, opened our windows, breathed in the fresh fragrances around us, and talked about the days ahead. He just knew he would be the first to die because of his age, so his place would be "next" in the family lineup, and Mrs. H would be to his left. Or so he thought.

With so much expense invested in preparing for death, he wanted to make sure someone would come and visit from time to time, making the purchase of such a serene resting place worth it. I promised him that I would come by and make sure that the graves were visited. He seemed so amazed, comforted, and genuinely relieved that I had given my word. I knew how important this was for him at that moment.

Mr. and Mrs. H were solid Christians, so I was not concerned about their going straight to Heaven when their names were called. And called they were. She went first, and he joined her exactly a week later. I firmly believe he died of a broken heart. Life was impossible without the love of his life and the wife of his youth.

And yes, I kept my word to visit their bodies at their burial ground a month after their spirits were lifted up to be with the Lover of their souls. I sat and cried as I remembered with such fondness these two darling sweethearts. I remembered him telling me that he would be placed on the right and she would be placed next and realized that God had other plans. As I looked upon "them," it was the sweetest picture of how they slept in their bed at home: her on the right, and him on the left.

It was such a privilege to serve Mr. and Mrs. H in that last chapter before perfection overtook them.

DAD

Let's face it: there are times in life when we feel down and disconnected from people we love. Sometimes we desire to see people who no longer live nearby, or we want to hang out with folks but can't find time in our packed schedules. We especially yearn for those we love who have died. We will not be seeing them or hearing from them today. And that hurts. We long for that connection, but we must wait for the pain to subside.

Both Ron and I have spent many years away from our beloved family members. And we miss them, especially Dad. My father was escorted to Heaven on November 5, 2002. Dad was one of my very best friends, the greatest counselor, and so easy to be around. He was a fine Christian gentleman, a great husband to Mom, a dedicated and loyal worker, a great provider, and of course a wonderful father to his four kids. After losing his father at age twelve, he would have had every excuse to become a poor father, as he had no role model. Not him. He always took the high road. He made a decision to watch others and see what was worth imitating and applied that.

When we were living in Germany, my sisters and I would frequent Walter's (there is no "w" sound in German, so it was pronounced with a "v" sound). Walter's was a "public living room" tavern, down the street from where we lived. The community would gather nightly, drinking their beer, chatting, relaxing, and meeting new neighbors. We young *frauleins* loved to get out of the house and go practice our German — especially with the handsome boys. Silly girls.

If we were not home at a respectable hour, Dad would happen to "need a candy bar" around 11:00 PM, so he could walk down the street and check on his daughters. Walter's had a little window at the front of the building that permitted the customer to look into the back living room area while making a purchase. We, in our typical childlike fashion, referred to Dad in code. He was "the eagle" on certain days. Most of the time we felt like he parented in a fitting and fair manner. But buying a Snickers bar at midnight? Come on, Dad! Now that I am a parent, though, I understand his compelling love and desire to protect his three, dear American maidens in that uncharted, foreign establishment.

I miss those days, and I miss him. My older sister, Carole, has often seen eagles flying in the wild and has commented on how she felt Dad a little closer those days. There was one day when an eagle had landed on her back deck shortly after Dad had been called Home. It took her breath away; Dad was still checking on his girl.

Although I have never had an eagle visit me, I adjusted Dad from an eagle to a hawk, so I can feel close to him too. Every time a hawk comes to visit — and there have been a few times they have come to the fence, tree, or deck — I find myself remembering and missing Dad. There is something so grand about an eagle, but I am very taken when a hawk flies in for a short visit also. They keep me close to Dad's memory, and they too have great vision.

One time Ron and I had received a pair of free tickets to see the Ink and Blood exhibit in Lexington, Kentucky. Delighted to have the opportunity, we visited the display on one of Ron's days off. Gazing upon authentic Dead Sea Scrolls and pages from Gutenberg's original Bible, printed in the 1400s, touched my spirit heartily. Personally, the scroll fragments of Isaiah and Jeremiah were of particular significance, even though I was unable to read the Hebrew text. These were the very words of God to man. Astounding! The ink of the scribes and printers and the blood of the martyrs had been preserved for my eyes to behold. It was awe-inspiring.

As we were preparing to head home, Ron stopped in the bathroom while I lingered in the hallway. A man from far off started walking in my direction. As he approached me, I greeted him; all of the sudden, I felt like I was looking into the eyes of my father! In no other way did he resemble my father, but as we walked in opposing directions, I could barely breathe. His eyes were identical to Dad's — that soft, tired blue color that belonged to him alone. The man had looked right through me! What on earth had just taken place? As I reached the end of the hallway I turned around to catch one last glimpse of his back. He had stopped, turned around, and watched me retreat. As soon as I caught him looking at me, he turned and walked away. I was trembling; hands shaking, heart beating outside of my chest.

I found myself muttering, "I'm good, Dad; thanks for checking."

Now, of course, I am not saying I encountered my Dad that day: Scripture does not support that theory. But the closeness to him I felt that afternoon was unparalleled by anything else I have ever experienced. Nor is he appearing in the form of an eagle or hawk, but the sensation of his nearness at those particular times is breathtaking. They are gifts from our heavenly Father (capital F on that one) that He loves to shower His children with, ones I particularly love to receive!

My father suffered from macular degeneration that rendered him blind in his mid-seventies. Not a complaint came from his mouth. He had signed on to love, trust, and worship God regardless of any challenges that came his way. I remember him stating, "God gave me sight for seventy-six years, and for that I am most grateful."

Mom selected "Mine Eyes Have Seen the Glory" to sing at Dad's funeral. Truly they have! Every time I hear this wonderful song, I remember Dad's funeral. And I still cry when I hear it today.

We were all given an opportunity to speak at Dad's funeral but I declined. The wound was too fresh, the emotions too raw. Although all of us would have wanted to say something in tribute, Joanne, the youngest, took the time to write a letter which was read aloud by the officiant. In the days ahead, I wondered if I had made the right choice not to participate.

Within three weeks of traveling back to Kentucky, I was approached by one of our church leaders asking if I would be willing to deliver a one-minute tribute to my father for our Wednesday evening Thanksgiving service. Even though I was scared, I accepted, as I was sure God had given me another chance to give honor to Dad. I would deliver it this time. The Lord blessed that step of obedience. Fear gave way to faith that evening.

Thank you for your strong witness, Dad. What a class act! I know where you are, and I will soon be with you again, thanks be to Jesus, who made a way for us.

SPA FOR THE SOUL

We were hosting a women's event at our church, and I was asked to present "The Manicure" part of the spa treatment. My friend, Fay, provided the adornment, and Linda made the room look elegant and welcoming.

In preparing for my message, I thought, *What are some uses for our hands? Patting a dog, holding hands with someone you love, making bread, directing an orchestra, turning the pages of a Bible, playing a trumpet, typing an email, playing Charades, brushing your teeth, making your bed...*

Some people don't like the look of their hands. We need to be challenged to look beyond wrinkles, liver spots, or imperfections and see what our hands can do for us and others. I thought we needed to appreciate the fact that our hands have done so much for us over the years. Just think of what life would be like with no hands. Who would button your blouse or tie your shoes? Who would comb your hair the right way? Wouldn't you want to pull up your own underwear?

Human hands consist of a palm, five digits, and a wrist. The thumb can rotate ninety degrees, fingers about forty-five.

There are twenty-seven bones in our hand. That's a pretty complex design.

Some common phrases involving hands are. "I know it like the back of my hand," "That is second-hand information," and "He's my right-hand man." There is even a whole language using hands: sign language. Clocks have hands. Hands are used as a unit of measurement for determining the height of horses. Hands truly are an important part of our lives.

One of the Scriptures I used for this event was Galatians 2:20: "I have been crucified with Christ and I no longer live, but Christ lives in me. The life I live in the body, I live by faith in the Son of God, who loved me and gave Himself for me."

So, you see, our hands are not really our hands—they're His hands. What does He want to accomplish with those hands of His through you? Maybe it's writing a note of encouragement to someone who needs it. It could be giving a hug to a person you have been at odds with for far too long. How about serving a tired family member? Every time you look at your hands, ask Him how He'd like you to use them for His glory. He has even left the "nails" in those hands of yours, so we can never forget!

As I was preparing for this talk, I noticed the front page of the *Courier-Journal* one morning and recognized a very handsome young man jumping for joy: it was none other than our son, Scott. He was the long snapper for the Louisville Male High School football team, and they had just won a huge victory over St. Xavier in the final seconds of the game. Scott had expeditiously and perfectly snapped the football to Matt, the holder, who placed it for Richard for the winning kick. Jubilant was an understatement of what this picture expressed. Scott is 6'4" and was jumping high in the air. Richard is smaller in stature, which made Scott's leap look even higher. But their faces tell all: snapper and kicker made magic!

As God was teaching me about hands, I could not help but notice Scott's beautiful, gentle hands. One is over Richard's chest (heart area) and the other endearingly wrapping itself around Richard's helmet (head). It struck me as a "divine picture." How beautiful those hands — the ones that snapped the winning field goal. Wow, what a great gift. Nothing happens by chance. Everything by His grace.

MOONSCAPE

I have always loved the moon — it is such a romantic image in my head. People say they "love you to the moon" while others wish they could "send you to the moon." It represents creation, strength, enormity, distance, and constancy; even when eclipsed, we know it's there. It can be seen from every corner of this planet. Well, actually, something round probably doesn't have corners, but you get my drift.

King David called the moon "a faithful witness in the sky." Don't you just love that description? He wrote that in Psalm 89. It's my favorite description of the moon.

Genesis 1 records that on the fourth day of creation God said, "Let there be lights in the expanse of the sky to separate the day from the night." And it was so. God made the two great lights — the greater light to have dominion over the day and the lesser light to have dominion over the night — as well as the stars. God placed them in the expanse of the sky to provide light on the earth.

Because I am one of the soundest sleepers on planet earth, I was shocked I was up one night at 2:30 AM and could not go back to sleep. How aggravating! Some people have serious issues sleeping. I am not one of them. But that particular night I could not stop tossing, turning, and fluffing the pillow, adding more blankets, taking off blankets, even praying for sleep, but nothing would bring the Sand Man that night. Nothing.

So as not to awaken Ron, I slipped out of bed after about thirty minutes and sat on the couch, frustrated and grumpy. Then I drew open the blinds and saw the most beautiful moonscape I had ever seen, a full moon that seemed to be only a neighbor's yard away. It was sooooo close. And huge. And brilliant. Just the right amount of clouds were passing it at just the right speed. It was like God was inviting me to join Him: "Hey Nancy, I didn't want you to miss this..." Glory be!

I had to be outside. With robe and slippers on, I sat on the back patio and was inspired to pray: "You, oh Lord, are truly the 'bright Morning Star,' as it says in Revelation 22:16. So bright, and powerful, and constant, and faithful, and beautiful, just like this gorgeous moon. Even the clouds would like to hide You from me, even if for only a few moments. But I know You are there. The clouds are like the storms of life that come and go. But Your presence is unchanging, faithful, and strong."

It was such a gift addressing Him as the *bright* (brightest moon ever) *Morning* (it was after midnight), *Star* (although the moon is not a star, the sun is, and that's what reflects off the moon, giving it light). It was an incredible time of worship.

O Mighty Maker of Heaven, Earth, and everything in them, I love You so much.

TIME FOR PRAYER

O ne season of life was devoted to teaching at a small college. At about the three-year mark, I was pretty well-known on campus, having had many hundreds of the students in my classroom.

One day, students started filing in before the appointed time of class: 8:30 AM. One otherwise spunky gal, Lisa, entered the classroom with the weight of the world on her shoulders. Her face was downcast, her shoulders slumped, her gait more of a shuffle. I quietly asked her what was wrong. She divulged that her very dear grandmother had died that morning. Her grades were important to her, so she was attempting to soldier through her sadness that day at school.

The Lord impressed upon me to pray for her. *Right here? Right now?* Of course I would pray for her, but could we do this later? *After class?* I asked God. *Now,* was His solid response. *Yes Sir.* Knowing this could be a fast route to being fired at a public college, I gave thought to the consequences a full ten seconds. But I decided I must listen to the Voice of Authority in my life, come what may.

When all my students were seated and no further interruptions would be forthcoming, I softly welcomed the class and informed them that Lisa had just lost her grandmother. I said that we would be offering a prayer for God to bring her comfort, peace, and focus for the next few hours. You could have heard a pin drop. Not a creature was stirring, not even a mouse. (Yes, we once discovered a mouse in that very classroom, but not that day.)

I boldly brought her before the Throne of Grace, asking for Him to do what He does: bring strength, peace, and help to those who ask. After a few moments of petitioning and praising, I prayed in the Name of my Savior, Jesus Christ.

From the back corner of the still room came a fist pump, and the booming voice of Tiffany: "Why, Ms. Nancy, I didn't think anyone did that anymore. Thank you so much!" What great confirmation to hear that dear lady give consent. If everyone else complained to Student Services, I would walk forward with head held high on the narrow road that so few find. He is faithful. Lisa was a changed lady that day. God had indeed helped her get through that class.

And no one said one thing against that prayer offered in sincere faith that day. Until freedom is taken from us, we should be willing to pray whenever and wherever we can. Such a privilege I will never take for granted.

PEDICURES TO SALVATION

A few weeks after leaving the small college where I taught for almost four years, God made His next move known to me. One day I had gone to my nail salon for a pedicure, where Louis, the gentleman who does the most amazing job on feet I have ever known, cuts, shapes, and paints my nails. It is total transformation. We have known one another for years. This particular day he approached me and asked me if I would consider teaching his kids and a few others. When asked what he would like taught, he simply responded, "Anything you want." *Well, that certainly narrows it down.*

Not sure if it was God or Louis speaking, I made my way to the drying station to have a little conversation with the Lord. It went something like this:

Me: "Is this You speaking, Lord? What shall I teach them?"

Him: "Nancy, what is your favorite subject?"

Me: "Well, You know it's the Bible."

Him: Silence…

After about fifteen minutes I made my way back to my friend, with my proposition. "Louis, I would love to teach your kids and others the Bible." I knew his response would make or break the opportunity set before me; he thought for a moment and proudly said, "Okay." Now I knew I was standing on holy ground. The Lord had indeed spoken. I know this devoted dad was thinking Math, Language Arts, and English, so I also added those subjects, too. But the privilege of teaching the Bible to others has always been the greatest privilege I could hope to have come my way.

Two weeks later five beautiful Vietnamese-American children were sitting at my kitchen table, representing grades three through eight. They were given their binders, grade-appropriate lessons, and brand-new Bibles. We began the first week with Genesis, the great place of beginnings, and overviewed a book each week. These children read God's Word, played games to review, and answered questions relative to the week's lesson. Imagine hearing the name Goliath for the first time and having to retain it. They were eager and adorable students.

We soon reached the Book of Joel. A recurring phrase from that Book is "The Day of the Lord." As I used that phrase over and over, Kenzie asked, "What does 'The Day of the Lord' mean?"

"I am so glad you asked, Kenzie!" was my response.

I told her that when Jesus came the first time, it was to die for our sins. His return trip would be a day of triumph for those found in Christ and a time of terror for those found not to be. In a very factual approach I laid out the two decisions that lay before mankind: to claim Him as Savior and Lord or to reject Him and suffer the consequences. Her smart, eight-year-old level head said she wanted to join the Army of God and be saved from eternal punishment. We all prayed with heads bowed that day as Kenzie invited Jesus into her tender heart. Hallelujah, what a Savior!

So that is how a pedicure can lead to salvation. Oh, I just looked at my feet; I think I need to call on Louis to perform his magic again.

QUEEN ESTHER

I have had the distinct pleasure of tutoring five Vietnamese-American elementary children in some of the basics of education. We have studied math, geography, language arts, science, and the Bible. I always tried to serve a snack that somehow related to the Books of the Bible we were studying. In Genesis we had animal crackers to commemorate God's creation of all creatures. In Exodus we had blue Gatorade and goldfish crackers because God divided the Red Sea to allow the Israelites safe passage. In Leviticus we snacked on red licorice, remembering the animal blood spilled to cover our sins. And so forth.

We were in the Book of Esther this particular week, and I served my students Veggie Straws. We ate and discussed the great story about this Jewish queen. Guessing "why" each particular snack was served had become a sort of competition between the students. Each wanted to be the first to make the connection with the snack and the story.

Just then I saw Rie look back one page in her notes to find that unfamiliar word "scepter" that she had never heard before and shouted out, "They are scepters!" Perfect. Yes, they are.

The king extended the scepter to his queen, welcoming her to speak with him. Don't you love fresh minds, new words, great stories, and smart kids? I sure do. I am blessed to be part of their young lives.

THE CASH CAB

You know the old television show, right? It involves a cab driver picking up unsuspecting travelers in New York City. He then presents them with random challenging questions. Some players earned free cab rides while others earned thousands of added dollars if they answered the questions correctly.

Our twenty-seven-year-old daughter had just received the devastating diagnosis of breast cancer, so I headed to Memphis to be with her during her procedure and recovery time. It was a very difficult time for our family, and we just needed a little pick-me-up.

After cabin fever had set in, I asked Becky if she would like to get out and perhaps go to lunch somewhere. She was all for that. As soon as we got into my car and shut the doors, I made the proclamation, "Welcome to the Cash Cab!" just like the cabbie in the beginning of his show. Becky was shocked and delighted. She immediately texted her brother in Louisville that she was in the Cash Cab. Of course it made no sense to him at all.

I asked her my random question, in exchange for lunch at McAlister's. CORRECT! We ate, we enjoyed, and we felt a little happier. We returned to my "cab" for another question. This one would entitle her to a new winter jacket that she desperately needed. CORRECT, and on to Burlington Coat Factory we went. And so progressed the fun afternoon. Breast cancer is diminished when joy overrules. She answered every carefully selected question correctly, giving us an unforgettable afternoon.

Several months later, Scott was going through a difficult time. I asked him if he wanted to hang out for the afternoon. He said that would be great. I went over to his apartment to pick him up. As soon as he closed the car door, he heard the familiar words, "Welcome to the Cash Cab!" He immediately texted his sister in Tennessee, and his great afternoon began.

I had selected seven rather difficult questions from random categories: politics, sports, science, the Bible, music, and pop culture. Every question had a "destination" assigned to it. I knew he wanted that new pair of sneakers, so when he drew that question, I said, "Oh, huge pressure on this one, son; you will so want this." Of course he had no idea what he was trying to win at the time, and I had not driven to the destination yet. He carefully weighed all the possible answers out loud so as not to make a mistake. The verbal conversation he had with himself gave great insight into his thought process. He eliminated one after another until he had made his final choice. No going back. Well, if he didn't get every one of them correct, too! These kids are costing us. And so, lunch was served, sneakers were purchased, a book was chosen, groceries selected, and gifts were adding up.

Jesus tells us it is more blessed to give than receive. I second that. Truly, I had the time of my life with those two dear kids those two afternoons. Thanks, Mr. Cabbie. What a great idea for blessing those who need a little blessing.

NIGHTSHIRTS

There are just some amusing trends that start from nowhere, like naming inanimate objects. I don't know how they start—or how to stop them. Naming cars is popular, as we are often in them and love them so much. Our family has had Freddy the Fore Runner, Sally the Saturn, Ethel the Explorer, and Sterling the Super Sport. But who on earth would name a nightshirt? Well, me of course.

One morning as I was frying what seemed to be a pound of bacon for breakfast, I realized that all the bacon grease seemed to attach itself to my bluish nightshirt. Hours later I still smelled like bacon. I know tossing the nightshirt in the laundry chute, taking a shower, and selecting another outfit may have corrected things—but no, I named my first nightshirt "Greaseball" and went on with that laughable, lazy Saturday.

A few months later I found myself in a two-piece summer pajama ensemble called "Fruit Cocktail." And on the heels of that, there was "Orange Sherbet."

I was visiting family in Boston one year and heard my father say, "Big Heart, come over here." I looked at the nightshirt I was wearing, a white knitted gown with red trim along the bottom and a huge red heart on the chest. Oh no, now others were naming them for me! How did this cat get out of the bag? Oh yes, because we were all enjoying ourselves.

Winter wear consisted of a new fashionable gown called "Polar Express," and gray, black, and red pajamas named "Penguins."

As one of my Bible study gals was recovering from a hysterectomy in the last quarter of the year, we disciples decided to make our healing friend feel more comfortable by wearing our pajamas to her place and having a meal with her. I selected my warmest fleece set, as I would be driving over "dressed" for this uproarious event..."Grease Fleece" was selected for that outing. Thankfully everyone drove the speed limit, and no broken tail lights were reported. We graciously spared the police another crazy incident report.

"Cloudball" was selected to fly to Poland, and "Christmas in New England" was chosen to make a trip to Pigeon Forge. "Garden Isle" was purchased with an upcoming trip to Hawaii in mind. "Lotsa Love" has made several trips to Boston.

With such a quirky fixation on naming nighties, it was determined that I would buy something I liked and the family and a few close friends would have a naming competition. The nightshirt I selected was the quintessential white gown with thin green stripes all the way around and down to the hem. There was a small bow at the neckline. Sixteen possible winners were randomly thrown into a bowl. Names like: "John Deere," "Thin Mint" (gotta love a 3X gown called "thin"), "Grasshopper," and "Emerald City." But the winner during this contest was hands down "Green Hornet." And on it goes...

You know when you have a favorite article of clothing that just won't die? Won't tear? Won't shrink? The one you wear over and over for years and years? Well, "Threadbare" had to be parted with at some point. It was a sleeveless summer beauty, brilliantly smocked and handsomely designed. Before disposing of it, I wondered if it should be downgraded to a dust rag or something. But as I considered it, there wasn't enough cloth to even dust with! Nope, decision made. Such sadness enveloped me. Now parting with it may not have made such an impression if I hadn't named it, right? Oh for goodness sake, let's go out shopping and buy "Squirrel." And it was so.

After Becky was married for a few months, her husband, Mike, named her long white old fashioned nightgown "Ebeneezer" from *A Christmas Carol*. These laughs were now generational! So a few years ago Becky and I decided to make a new Christmas tradition. She would buy me a new nightshirt, and I would buy one for her. The only catch was that it had to be the worst possible nightwear we could find.

The last gift to be opened on Christmas Eve was the nightshirt exchange. I opened the most hideously brightly colored, Japanese looking, bizarrely patterned, gauze-like piece of material. Oh my! Never in all of my days would I have ever chosen this gem. It was the perfect gift. Now to name it. Again, all family members put their two cents in, and "Kim-Mo-NO" was named, Emphasis on NO. Haaaaaa!

The newlywed received the worst old lady gown ever. She put it on and truly looked a hundred years old. Smashing success! She named hers "Vovo," which was her great grand-mother's name of affection.

This past Christmas, "Tsunami" was gifted me—a poly-ester blend with bold blue and black waves. If you have a problem with vertigo, you may not wish to look at it directly for too long. And I don't think it glows in the dark, but I'm not absolutely sure .

We've have had some real winners already. I am looking forward to December. If you see Becky at a bargain table in the women's department, let her be. She's making another great selection for her mother!

BEING MORE AMISH

Do you ever find yourself running faster and faster, undertaking more and more projects or tasks, while the most important things in life go unattended? Many enter the distracted life or a life of busyness quite unintentionally. Certain things are entertained because we are good at something, or because they catch our eye and we're interested, or we are available. But when you break down the twenty-four-hour days we have been assigned, oftentimes we find imbalances. At least that is true in my life. Paul laments, "Why do I do the things I don't want to do and don't do the things I want to do?" I share your sentiments, Paul.

God got my attention in a pretty big way when my dear friend Elizabeth gave me the book *Almost Amish* by Nancy Sleeth. Nancy very practically tells her compelling story toward a simpler, more sustainable life. The remedy I was seeking. Everyone does "simpler" a little differently, so mine looked my way.

I started decluttering our house and joyfully gave things away that needed to go to another good home. How liberating to bag up lost-now-found treasures and part with things we no longer needed. Time for someone else to enjoy them for the next season. And then I moved on to decluttering my life.

Homemade bread was another delicious addition to our new lifestyle. My sister had given us a bread machine some years ago, so I went back to baking fresh bread and found some new recipes like Portuguese sweet bread, one of Ron's favorites, and Italian herb, our son's favorite. The smell of fresh bread baking in a home is quite delightful — and filling.

We recognized that many great friendships had been put on hold due to other priorities, so we changed that too. We started our "Almost Amish" dinners, inviting two to four people to our table to dine and catch up. I made simple, affordable meals and usually gave leftovers to our guests for another meal for them to enjoy. How great it is to gather at the table with people you love, enjoy some good nourishment, and share stories that entertain or create some uncontrollable laughter.

In line with some of these changes, I made the decision to stop teaching at the local college. More and more demands were being made of us, and I felt it was time to tender my resignation. I have missed part of that life but truly enjoy this lifestyle so much more. There is more in less on all levels. Like Paul, I am learning the secret of being content. Time is a most precious commodity, a gift that only so much is given to each of us. I am learning to number my days aright.

Yes, I still enjoy my phone, my iPad, my car, and a variety of other luxuries, so I am not exactly Amish. But, as Nancy Sleeth says, I am "Almost Amish."

MS. NERMA

There was once a darling lady named Nerma. I would look after her now and again, when her daughter was serving the Lord in a number of ways or visiting out-of-town family. I watched Nerma graduate from ninety-four grace-filled years to ninety-six, and I considered it a privilege to do for her some things she was no longer able to do for herself.

Nerma had a wonderful personality; no one disliked Ms. Nerma. She captured and mastered the beauty of simplicity. She was an artsy gal with a comedic approach to life, a musician, and one who cared deeply for the other guy, whoever the other guy may have been.

Looking through old pictures with her told me much of her life's story. Having lost much in her ninety-six years, there seemed to be a greater sweetness to her game.

One night after I had doled out a very generous snack of two teeny, tiny mini teddy grahams before bed time, she looked across the room to where I was seated and offered me one of her prized snacks. That generation, I tell you! They penetrate us with the spirit of humility (almost) every single time, searing our hearts. Two tiny crackers received; one to be given away? When do these thoughts become routine in one's life? I must know.

God was generous in giving us His Son. Following Jesus and trusting Him implicitly while dying to self brings about this character that is so attractive. For God so loved us that He gave us Jesus Christ!

Nerma, thanks so much for the many great lessons in helping to grow me more into the image of Christ.

THE TRAFFICKED

A few years ago the Lord prompted me to consider looking into the sexually trafficked epidemic in our world. When you look at the travesty of modern-day slavery in any form, you will be forever changed. I began to volunteer with a local ministry that feeds, loves, mentors, and teaches those who have left or are hoping to leave the adult entertainment industry. Every lady is created in His image and has been given purpose, hope, and a future because of the finished work of Jesus Christ. Oh, the glory He receives from His beloved princesses! Here is one such encounter.

I was on assignment a short time ago, caring for a ninety-six-year-old friend, when I received a phone call from one our ladies at the ministry, MC. She called to discuss some difficult things she needed to talk through.

I invited MC over so we could discuss her concerns, resolve the issues we could, pray for freedom and releases, and fellowship. She made her way over in very short order.

MC loves coffee, so I made her a cup. She curled up on the floor, by the couch I was sitting on and faced the great outdoors.

She began to share from her heavy heart. As we talked openly, I found myself reaching for my Bible, the source of all truth. We had previously briefly discussed the well-known man given so many trials to deal with, Job.

I began to read from Job 38, telling MC that for 37 chapters all the characters had been chatting on about all sorts of things. But in Chapter 38 I read, "Then the Lord answered Job from the whirlwind: 'Who is this that questions my wisdom with such ignorant words? Brace yourself like a man, because I have some questions for you, and you must answer them'…"

MC's response was one of astonishment: "Did God really say that?" She had never read the latter part of Job. And as we went on for the next few moments, wondering what it would feel like to be asked questions like that by God, we realized the eternal greatness of God and the smallness of man. We confessed we were *not* around when He laid the foundations of the earth. Nor did we have anything to do with giving the horse his strength. It was a nice wake-up call.

With each chapter He became bigger and bigger, and we found our rightful places, under His supremacy and celebrating His awesomeness. All of creation was doing what it was told. Wind, come in at five miles per hour from the northwest. And it was so. Frog, jump. And he does. Stones crying out if called upon. Such order and obedience, under the authority of the Creator. All but the crown jewel of creation: mankind, free to obey, free to disobey.

MC looked through the glass door to a majestic oak, and simply remarked, "So that tree is more obedient than I am, right? He says for it to stand, and it does. And it brings Him glory in the process."

She won the Student of the Hour award that day. Simple, yet profound. No tree is going to outperform her!

JADE BRACELETS

While visiting family in Hawaii one year, our niece Robin approached us on Saturday night and asked if we planned to attend church in the morning. I responded, "Yes, Robin, would you like to join us?" She accepted, and we were delighted. I had known Robin for thirty-five years, and this was the first time she asked to accompany us.

The next morning we arrived at the church we attend when we are in town. Robin's daughter Nicole attended the high school group while the adults went into the sanctuary to find seats.

The guest preacher that day was from South America; he had been educated in the Pacific Northwest and was visiting an outer Hawaiian island for the very first time. And we are people who hardly ever attend this church but were in attendance that particular week. I think of the great lengths God goes to meet us and am constantly stunned. How deeply He cares for us.

Robin, thirty-eight, sat between Uncle and Aunty that day. At the end of the service the preacher asked us to bow our heads and give our lives to Jesus, if we were so inclined, and to admit we had asked Jesus into our hearts by raising a hand. We all recited the prayer of confession aloud.

I thought I heard the clanging of Robin's two jade bracelets, which would have indicated that she had said "yes" to Jesus. (Ron later said he heard and thought the same thing). And so it was.

As we were leaving the church service, Robin approached the "Yes" table at the rear of the sanctuary and took a Bible. I then needed to know. "Did you accept Jesus today?"

A simple "Yes, Aunty," was her response. *Well hallelujah, what a Savior! I have been praying for this dear child for years.*

She read late into the night and had finished all of Genesis and half of Exodus by the next day. She is now studying online for a Christian Counseling degree, and I cannot be more proud of her. Oh, the things He has rescued her from. There is peace, guidance, hope, love, and joy in her step today. Again, Jesus makes all the difference.

MOM

My mother was born to hard-working Swedish immigrants. Her parents arrived in America in 1905, got married, and had seven children. Mother was the baby. She was a fun-loving extrovert who was generous and kind. She kept a clean house; food was always cooked by hand, served on time, and everything was always in its place. She learned order from her mother — my grandmother, Mammy. Mom had a great sense of humor, and she loved to celebrate every occasion that came along.

Every day had purpose. Mondays were spent cleaning the house, Tuesdays were set aside for laundry for the six members of our household, Wednesday was ironing day, and Thursdays were reserved for a trip to the neighboring town for the weekly grocery shopping and trips to a discounted clothing store. Saturdays and Sundays were off days, and we always visited the grandparents and caught up with their lives. I loved and appreciated her schedule. It kept things regular and in rhythm. I never remember her running out of milk and always had ironed, clean clothes to wear. Oh, that I had the discipline of that woman today.

Three of us girls slept in the same room — a set of bunk beds for the two younger girls, and a twin bed for our older sister. Most Thursdays I would come home from school and find clothes beautifully laid out on the bed. It might have been a dress or a pair of socks. It was a gift, and it was new, and it was mine. That messaging to me was golden; while I was working in school, she was thinking of me and reflected those thoughts with generous gifts when I walked through the door. What a sweet, thoughtful, kind-hearted gesture. I loved coming into my room Thursday afternoons, knowing a gift would be waiting for me.

Mother met God in 1979. She had never been churched a day in her life. When her older sister was diagnosed with breast cancer, she thought to look for answers in a church close to home, and she found Jesus. He changed everything. She could not help but share Him with the rest of the family. We all trust Him today because of her bold decision to look for the reason and purpose of life during that dark period. Had she never entered the door of that church and met those wonderful people that day, I shudder to think where spiritual things might be with our family today.

Mom and Dad always had a great marriage and a firm commitment toward family. The older I become, the more I really appreciate that gift. Wheels were set in motion for us at an early age, and we are all most grateful. But after Mom and Dad met Jesus and developed a solid faith, they were even kinder and sweeter with age. Grace entered the picture, and we all could see it.

After Dad went Home to glory, Mom continued to live out her days, missing him terribly. One day, she was walking with a friend and tripped and fell, breaking her hip. She underwent surgery and was placed in a rehab facility for a time. The testing of her mental faculties proved her to be in need of further assistance, so she stayed at the facility. Her doctors agreed it was the safest place for her. The family agreed with the professional advice.

I was up in Boston for a family visit and was voted to be the one to tell her she was not going home after all, but would be staying where she currently was. Not an easy task. No one wants to hear that, and no one wants to be the emissary of that edict, either.

As I visited with her that afternoon, I told her as gently as I could what the plan was, knowing she was working so hard to get back to her home. I dreaded telling her the decision, and worried that she would be hurt by it. Her simple response? "Well, if that's the way it has to be . " After we said our goodbyes that day, I found myself in my sister's car in the parking lot of the nursing home. I cried for twenty minutes, and then broke the silence by saying, "What a woman of grace my mother is!" Gratitude and grace always break my heart. How could this brokenhearted senior respond with such acceptance? Such ease? Grace is my only answer. God's grace poured out of Himself, onto her and onto me so generously that afternoon. What a lesson I learned that day of a faith-filled woman who had her eyes on higher heights than self.

Mom and Dad are now together again, living in perfection. I can't wait to be with them again. As their headstone reads,

"Together Forever". And you can take that truth to the bank. They are both enjoying a place where sin is no more.

Thanks, Mom, for living, loving, instructing, and finishing well.

GRANDPARENTING

"Oh just you wait, Nancy!"

"There is nothing like it!"

"It's the greatest gift you could ever hope for!"

"You will never be the same again!"

These are the phrases I have heard for years from friends who entered the season of grandparenting earlier than we did. Well, maybe we were a little late to the party, but we are here now. And I must say, "It is *grand!*"

Ron and I traveled to Atlanta, about a seven-hour journey, anticipating the glorious arrival of our grandson. Becky was to be induced at 8:00 AM the next morning, so we arrived the evening before and embraced our over-ready, very pregnant daughter.

As we talked through some fears and apprehensions young marrieds are apt to have about becoming parents, I asked Becky how she was feeling. She strolled through the living room without making eye contact and simply commented, "Dead woman walking."

In fairness to her lack of enthusiasm, no one knew definitively what the next day would bring. There are so many worries, concerns, pain, and unknowns with childbirth that it's difficult to find a quiet confidence in moving forward. The constant ticking of the clock seemed even louder. Getting to sleep that night was a struggle for all, yet excitement governed our hearts.

Mike and Becky made their way to the hospital thirty minutes sooner than the grandparents-in-waiting did. As we parked in the garage of Piedmont Hospital, we remembered with fondness the same trek we had made to that same hospital thirty-three years before to have our baby girl, Rebecca Lynn. Such are the gifts handed to us, if we take the time to unwrap them.

Ann, Mike's mother, made her way to the maternity section, and we jointly found our way to the parents-to-be. What a beautiful birthing room they had to welcome their son. We chatted, waited, prayed, and watched *Family Feud*, hoping we'd not be the next contestants.

As the Pitocin increased, so did Becky's contractions. Finally, it was time for the expectant couple to privately go to the place so many before them had gone: the miracle of birthing a baby. Knowing the gender took the guesswork out of the equation, but the timing was totally unknown.

Ten hours and seventeen minutes from the parking of the car in the hospital garage, our son-in-law stood before us in the waiting room and announced the arrival of his perfect son. We stood at attention, saluting the Author of Life and made our way to see the nine-month-in-coming little boy that God had knitted together in the secret place.

Behold, Silas Gordon Jarrell was in my arms within one hour of having left his mother's womb. Tears came in abundance and hearts swelled to twice their normal size as we beheld our glorious little gift, our first grandchild.

How can one tiny person change the world? If you already have one, you know. It is simply amazing. Silas Gordon is created in God's image and will accomplish, Lord willing, all God has designed for him to do.

He's cute. He's one of a kind. He's soft. He's cuddly. He learns every day. He responds. He laughs. What a delight he is to our family. How I love being his Nanny!